IMAGES
of America

SOUTHERN CALIFORNIA
TOP FUEL DRAGSTERS

IMAGES
of America

SOUTHERN CALIFORNIA
TOP FUEL DRAGSTERS

Steve Reyes

ARCADIA
PUBLISHING

Published by Arcadia Publishing
Charleston, South Carolina

Printed in the United States of America

Library of Congress Control Number: 2024931447

For all general information, please contact Arcadia Publishing:
Telephone 843-853-2070
Fax 843-853-0044
E-mail sales@arcadiapublishing.com

Visit us on the Internet at www.arcadiapublishing.com

To my "brothers" from another mother, Jamie and Sonny Jackson.
In memory of Jeff Jackson; son, father, drag racer. Gone but never forgotten.

CONTENTS

ACKNOWLEDGMENTS

Special thanks to Greg Sharp, Carl Olson, Dave Wallace Sr., Dave Wallace Jr., Don Gillespie, Phil Burgess (National Hot Rod Association [NHRA]), Geoff Stunkard (Quartermilestones), Bob "the Stat Guy" Frey, Lou Hart, and Bob Brown Photography for their help with this project. All photographs are from the archives of photographer Steve Reyes unless noted in the caption.

INTRODUCTION

Southern California was the undisputed birthplace of the sport of drag racing. The first organized drag race took place at the Santa Ana, California, airport around 1950. Thirteen years from its humble beginnings, drag racing crowned its king of the quarter mile, the front-engine top fuel dragster. With nitromethane as its fuel, the top fuel dragster became the quickest and fastest race in the world of automotive sports.

From a standing start, these land-bound missiles could cover a quarter mile at 300 feet per second and required a parachute and brakes to stop safely. The nitro-powered supercharged dragster made over 2,000 horsepower. Fearless drivers guided these "rail jobs" to smoke-filled 200-mile-per-hour runs down Southern California drag strips. Awestruck fans referred to these cars as "slingshots," "diggers," and of course "rail jobs."

Southern California was the place to prove how well your top fuel dragster stacked up against the best in the country. "SoCal" top fuel owners outnumbered the USA top fuel racers 10 to 1 so to be an outsider and win a top fuel event in SoCal was indeed a major accomplishment. Just to bring your car and qualify for a top fuel event was a challenge, and to win was the biggest challenge to any top fuel team.

With nitro fumes filling the air and smoke billowing off the huge slick-style rear tires, these local racers traversed the quarter mile side by side every weekend. Bakersfield all the way to San Diego hosted top fuel events on a weekly basis. The front-engine top fuel dragster thundered down Southern California drag strips from 1963 to 1971–1972; this would be considered the golden era of top fuel racing. For about nine years, the nitro-burning dragster ruled at Southern California drag strips.

The year 1971 saw the dawning of a modern style of top fuel dragster, the rear-engine top fuel dragster. This new/old innovation helped close the history of the front-engine top fuel dragster. But now with the trend of nostalgic-style drag racing that started in the early 1990s, the front-engine top fuel dragster has returned to drag racing in a big way. Across the United States, cars are being built or restored for nostalgic drag racing. There has been a 20-year hiatus for the front-engine fueler, but they are back at events like the California Hot Rod Reunion at Bakersfield in October or Steve Gibbs's Nitro Revival, which is held at Irwindale in November.

Once again, old-timers and newcomers can be delighted in watching the front-engine top fuel dragsters battle across the country's quarter-mile racetracks.

One

BLOOD, SWEAT, AND NITRO

The Santa Ana, California, airport held the first organized drag races on July 2, 1950. C.J. Hart, Creighton Hunter, and Frank Stillwell were partners who were responsible for bringing drag racing to a real place to race in Southern California. The track required a 50¢ admission fee and featured timing lights. There was even a snack bar for hungry fans and racers. Grandstands were available for spectators to watch all the quarter-mile action. The racetrack was open from 1950 to 1959, after which it went back to being part of the airport. (Courtesy of the Greg Sharp Collection.)

Lloyd Scott went for something different on May 5, 1955, by debuting his "Bustle Bomb" twin-engine race car. The car featured an Oldsmobile engine in the back and a Cadillac engine in front. Scott ran the first 150 miles per hour at Lawrenceville, Illinois. He raced down the quarter mile and was clocked at 151.01 miles per hour on regular pump gas. (Courtesy of the Greg Sharp Collection.)

Calvin Rice debuted his first race car in 1950. It was a 1932 Ford Coupe that ran 97 miles per hour in a quarter mile. Then in 1955, he was in a dragster-style race car. Calvin first used a Ford Flathead engine for power but wanted more horsepower. He switched to a Chrysler Hemi engine with nitromethane for fuel, there was no gasoline in his race car. In 1955, he won the first-ever NHRA US Nationals, which was held in Great Bend, Kansas. The following year, he won the first Bakersfield Championships with a speed of 156.46 miles per hour. (Courtesy of the Greg Sharp Collection.)

Fritz Voight not only raced his own slingshot-style dragster, but he also drove for Mickey Thompson. Fritz was runner-up to Calvin Rice at the 1955 Arizona National Championships. At that event, Rice ran his car on nitromethane, but Voight stayed with pump gas in his race car. At that point in drag racing, there were no restrictions on the type of fuel that could be used at NHRA events. It was all up to the owner/driver of the race car what fuel was used. (Courtesy of the Greg Sharp Collection.)

On April 11, 1953, NHRA had its first official sanctioned race at the Pomona fairgrounds complex in Pomona, California. In this photograph, two top eliminator racers squared off for the final race of the day. The car on the left is an Indy-style race car that had been converted for the drag strip. On the right is the modern style of a slingshot-designed race car. The slingshot design soon became the norm in the dragster class, with all other styles becoming outdated in Southern California drag racing. (Courtesy of the Greg Sharp Collection.)

11

On September 29, 1955, the first NHRA Nationals were held in Great Bend, Kansas. Two of the big names in Southern California drag racing raced for top honors in the final round. Calvin Rice and his "Riley and Sons" nitro-burning dragster went head-to-head with Mickey Thompson and his "Panorama City Special" dragster. Rice and his nitro burner prevailed over Thompson's pump gas-burning dragster. Thompson's Panorama City dragster was considered the first streamlined-style slingshot dragster in drag racing. The car featured a full body that covered the engine and rear wheels on the slingshot chassis. (Courtesy of the Greg Sharp Collection.)

"The King of Speed," Mickey Thompson, unveiled his first streamlined slingshot dragster in 1954. The sleek beauty was state of the art for 1954. Being the promoter/racer, Thompson arranged for the City of Panorama to sponsor his new venture so he could attend the 1955 NHRA Nationals in Great Bend, Kansas. The city leaders got their money's worth as Thompson was runner-up to Calvin Rice in top eliminator. The streamliner was featured in every automotive publication at the time, and it did not cost Thompson a single penny. (Courtesy of the Greg Sharp Collection.)

The shiny unlettered new Cook and Bedwell dragster was paired with Carlos Ramirez in the "Bean Bandits" dragster for photographer Bob Hardee. Emery Cook was behind the wheel of the Cook and Bedwell dragster. It was 1957, and both cars ran on nitromethane, which had become the norm for Southern California racers since 1952. An interesting note is that the first woman to drive a nitro-powered dragster came about in Gary, Indiana. On July 6, 1958, Lynne Sturmer drove the Bean Bandits nitro-burning dragster against an airplane at the Gary US 30 drag strip to promote the Cole Bros. Air Circus that had come to Gary, Indiana. (Courtesy of the Greg Sharp Collection.)

Just before NHRA's nitro ban, Emery Cook astounded the drag racing world with a 166.97-mile-per-hour blast at Lions Drag Strip in Wilmington, California, (Long Beach area) on February 3, 1957. Cook was driving the Cook and Bedwell "Isky U Fab Special" top fuel dragster, and he backed that up with a 165.13-mile-per-hour run the same day. That day, he became the fastest man in the sport of drag racing. (Courtesy of the Greg Sharp Collection.)

This jovial gentleman was Jim Deist, who was the first man to make parachutes for dragsters. He also made the first fire suits for drivers in the dragster classes. In 1959, Deist and his trusty sewing machine began to crank out parachutes to help stop the faster cars in drag racing. In his small Southern California shop, he put together some of the first fire suits and protective gear worn by dragster drivers. Deist's fire suits saved many a driver from very painful oil and nitro burns. Soon, other manufacturers of safety gear would follow Deist; Bill Simpson, Bob Filler, and Bob's Drag Chutes in the Midwest all designed and made products to save drivers from injury.

The first-ever Smokers Fuel and Gas Championships took place in Bakersfield, California. On March 5, 1959, going head-to-head, was Art Chrisman (nearside) versus Tony Waters (far side). Chrisman took home top honors as Waters's roadster got out of shape and had to shut off. Chrisman ran 9.36 at 140.50 miles per hour on that final run. Both were running nitromethane for fuel as Chrisman and Waters ignored the NHRA nitro ban. They were not the only ones. Many racers and racetracks in Southern California did as well. (Photograph by Bob Hardee; courtesy of the Greg Sharp Collection.)

At the 1959 Smokers Fuel and Gas Championships in Bakersfield, Gary Cagle had a top speed at the event of 180.36 miles per hour. Cagle and his state-of-the-art top fuel dragster headed to the Midwest/East to race. His tour was cut short when he crashed and destroyed his car in the Midwest. Cagle was beaten up and returned with his now wrecked racer to the West Coast to try and rebuild. He would return to the top fuel wars raging in Southern California with an all-new fueler. (Courtesy of the Greg Sharp Collection.)

Mickey Thompson not only drove land speed cars and dragsters, he was also the manager of Lions Drag Strip in Wilmington, California. Thompson was its first manager starting in 1955 when it opened. He was one of the big voices in drag racing who wanted a ban on nitromethane. He would concur with NHRA president Wally Parks about the dangers of nitro and concern for driver safety. His meetings with Parks worked as NHRA banned nitromethane as a racing fuel from 1957 to 1963. The ban was loosely enforced, with many Southern California racers and racetracks ignoring NHRA's ruling. Better safety equipment got the ban rescinded at the beginning of 1963. Florida's Don Garlits won the first official NHRA top fuel eliminator at the 1963 NHRA Winternationals held in Pomona, California. (Courtesy of the Don Gillespie Collection.)

Between 1957 and 1962, Dode Martin and "Jazzy" Jim Nelson made available a do-it-yourself dragster in kit form. Their Drag Master Company had quite a few well-known drag racers using their product. Some of their early customers were Mickey Thompson, Roland Leong, Danny Ongais, and Pete Robinson. Mickey Thompson, pictured in his "Drag Master" dragster, did very well with his, as did many racers all over the United States. Martin and Nelson did not just make these cars, but they also raced them. In fact, on June 10, 1962, Nelson set the top gas record at 8.67 ET (elapsed time) in Pomona, California. (Courtesy of the Greg Sharp Collection.)

Longtime race car driver/owner Leland Kolb was racing a Chrysler-powered 1932 roadster at Saugus, California, in 1954. At Fontana, California, in 1960, he was behind the wheel of the Duncan Built Homes top fuel dragster racing Chuck Gireth in the Gireth and Carpenter top fuel dragster. Gireth won this duel. Kolb kept racing in top fuel well into the 1970s. He gave young guns "Captain" Billy Tidwell and Kelly "the Controller" Brown the chance to drive a top fuel dragster in Southern California. (Courtesy of the Greg Sharp Collection.)

This was the top eliminator lineup at Lions Drag Strip in 1960. Seven cars competed for the top prize. However, there are only six drivers for the seven cars; Jack Chrisman (second from the right) was driving two cars that day ("the Howard Cam" twin bear and "the Magwinder"). Other notable drivers in this lineup were Hayden Proffitt and his dragster (far right), and mid-pack all the way from Chicago was Chris Karamesine's "Chizer" with John Krandenburg as the driver. (Courtesy of the Greg Sharp Collection.)

When one is the track manager like Mickey Thompson was at Lions, anything is possible. Here, in 1960, Fritz Voight was behind the wheel of one of Thompson's land speed cars doing a few test and tune passes of the twin Pontiac engine beast before heading to the Bonneville Salt Flats in Wendover, Utah. Thompson took over driving chores at Bonneville. (Courtesy of the Greg Sharp Collection.)

The Southern California top fuel racers hated to deal with one Chrisman Bros. and Cannon top fuel dragster, so how about two cars in 1962? Frank Cannon was at the controls of the very potent No. 2 car. Cannon soon struck out on his own with a whole line of "Hustler" top fuel cars in the 1960s. Cannon was a homer and raced in Southern California for most of his career. (Courtesy of the Greg Sharp Collection.)

It was a burned-up top fuel dragster that Tom Greer bought from top fuel racer Rod Stuckey in 1961. Stuckey had a major-league fire in his then new top fueler. Instead of repairing it, he unloaded it to Greer. Greer in turn took it to Kent Fuller, and Fuller worked his magic to restore the car back from the junk heap. Then Keith Black stepped in with one of his mighty Mopar Hemi engines for the old/new fueler. The car was painted, and all the details were taken care of; it was race-ready, but there was no driver for the restored fueler. Keith Black knew this kid from the San Fernando Valley and heard that he might be the guy he was looking for the fueler. A quick call to Don Prudhomme and the Greer and Black had a driver for its top fuel dragster. (Photograph by Kaye Trapp; courtesy of the Greg Sharp Collection.)

The King of Southern California's top fuel dragsters in the late 1950s and early 1960s was Art Chrisman. Chrisman driving the Chrisman Bros. and Cannon's "Hustler 1" top fuel dragster put fear into the heart of many a SoCal top fuel racer. At Lions Drag Strip, Chrisman made a tire-boiling run before the full body was added to the car. Autolite spark plugs became Chrisman's employer and major sponsor of the Hustler 1. (Courtesy of the Greg Sharp Collection.)

At Lions in 1962, the Greer, Black, and Prudhomme top fuel dragster started gathering wins at local SoCal drag strips. Because of business commitments, the team did not venture out of Southern California to race. From 1962 to 1964, the team victimized the local SoCal top fuel racers to the tune of 243 round wins to only 7 round losses. That total has been disputed as only 236 wins to 7 losses, regardless, either amount was quite the accomplishment that will probably stand forever. (Courtesy of the Greg Sharp Collection.)

This was a little bit of public relations for drag racing and top fuel dragsters at San Gabe in 1962. The Greer, Black, and Prudhomme top fuel dragster had a few admirers from *The Beverly Hillbillies* television show. Max Baer Jr. (Jethro) and Donna Douglas (Ellie May) checked out the top fueler while driver Don Prudhomme had an "aw, shucks" moment for the television stars and photographer. (Courtesy of the Greg Sharp Collection.)

At the 1962 NHRA US Nationals in Indianapolis, Jack Chrisman was driving for Mickey Thompson and his blown Pontiac top gas dragster. The following year, Chrisman switched rides to Vince Rossi's new top fuel dragster. Chrisman was seriously injured in Rossi's car at Pomona when the rear end spun because of broken chassis mounts. Doctors worked all night to save Chrisman's life, and because of his accident, changes were made to prevent this from happening again. Now a dragster chassis is required to include a Chrisman's cross, which is an extra brace to hold the rear housing in place and stop it from spinning. Chrisman recovered from his injuries and became the father of a new class in drag racing: the funny car. (Courtesy of the Dave Wallace Jr. Collection.)

"TV Tommy" Ivo and Rod Peppmuller combined their talents to build Ivo's first top fuel dragster, "the Barnstormer," in 1962. The car featured a blown nitro-burning Hemi built by Dave Zeuschel, and it also was a movie-star car. It appeared as one of the lead top fuel dragsters in the movie *Bikini Beach*. Ivo piloted his Barnstormer to the first sub-eight-second run in drag racing with a 7.99 ET at San Gabe in October 1962. That run made Ivo the quickest owner/driver on the West Coast. (Photograph by Jim Kelly; courtesy of the Greg Sharp Collection.)

It was 1963, and Tom McEwen is at the controls of the Broussard, Davis, and McEwen top fuel dragster. Even though it was early in McEwen's career, he had already driven about 15 top fuel and top gas dragsters. McEwen soon left this team and partnered with the Donovan and Dawes team to race in 1964. The Broussard and Davis fueler saw "the Flyin' Hawaiian" Danny Ongais fill the driver's seat of its "Mangler" top fuel dragster for 1964 and 1965. (Courtesy of the Greg Sharp Collection.)

At Pomona, California, in 1963, two members of the Road Kings Car Club did battle in top fuel dragsters: the Greer, Black, and Prudhomme top fueler, driven by Don Prudhomme (nearside), versus the Sour Sisters top fuel dragster, driven by Kenny Safford (far side). The Road Kings Car Club was formed in 1952 in Burbank, California. Some of its members were Tommy Ivo, Tom McCurry, Kenny Safford, Don Prudhomme, Don "the Beachcomber" Johnson, Bob Muravez (also known as Floyd Lippencott Jr.), Gary Cassidy, Don Gaide, Don Ratican, and chassis builders Roy Fjastad and Rod Peppmuller. (Courtesy of the Greg Sharp Collection.)

Bill Martin's 400 junior top fuel Chevrolet-powered dragster was the hardest-running Chevy-powered top fueler in Southern California from 1963 through 1965. Martin's drivers included Gary Cassidy (pictured), George Boltoff, Gary Gabelich, Butch Maas, and Mike Snively. All drove the car in a span of three years. The car was a familiar sight at any and all top fuel events in the 1963–1965 period. Martin could always be found racing at San Fernando on a Sunday afternoon. (Photograph by Dave Wallace Sr.)

Action at the "Pond," also known as the San Fernando Raceway, saw Bill Martin's 400 junior top fuel dragster with George Boltoff driving face off East Coast invader the Brooklyn, New York–based "Dead End Kids" top fuel dragster driven by "Rapid" Red Lang. Boltoff would send the Dead-End Kids back home with this round win. The Lang, Razon, Anahury, and Jeffers Dead End Kids top fueler was on tour after appearing on the cover of *Popular Mechanics* magazine in 1963. (Courtesy of the Dave Wallace Jr. Collection.)

From 1962 to 1964, the Greer, Black, and Prudhomme top fuel dragster was the car to beat in Southern California. Unfortunately, Tom Greer's financial woes spelled the end for the team in late 1964. With a lack of funds to race, Greer dropped out of the team. When the smoke cleared, Black came back with the car at the end of 1964. Not wanting to finance the car on his own or take time to find new monies, he parked the car, ending the reign of the Greer, Black, and Prudhomme top fuel dragster in Southern California. (Courtesy of the Greg Sharp Collection.)

"Stormin' Norman" Weekly, driving the Weekly, Rivero, Fox, and Holding "Frantic Four" top fuel dragster, raced the pride of Brooklyn, New York, the Dead End Kids top fuel dragster, with "Rapid" Red Lang at the controls. Norm Weekly, Ron Rivero, Jim Fox, and Dennis Holding formed their team in 1963. In 1963, the team won four of six top fuel events held at Pomona, California. They also beat the undefeatable Greer, Black, and Prudhomme, and their car was featured in the movie *Bikini Beach*. In addition, they appeared on the cover of Dick Dale's album cover in 1964. That same year, the foursome toured the United States match racing Florida's Don Garlits, Michigan's Connie Kalitta, Tommy Ivo, and Chicago's Chris Karamesines. (Courtesy of the Greg Sharp Collection.)

All the heavy hitters in Southern California top fuel racing got to appear in the *Bikini Beach* movie. Drag racing fans were treated to footage of SoCal top fuelers in action on the big screen nationwide. The movie brought drag racing into the lives of a lot of people throughout the United States and got people curious about the sport and all those long skinny fast racing cars. Even Tommy Ivo's four-engine "Showboat" was featured in this movie along with a whole slew of SoCal top fuelers. It was a major breakout for the sport and for top fuel dragsters.

"Jumpin' Jeep" Hampshire drove the Stellings and Hampshire "Red Stamp Special" top fuel dragster, and on February 4, 1964, he ran the first official NHRA sub-eight-second run at 7.97 ET at Pomona, California. Jeep also recorded the first unofficial 200-mile-per-hour run with the Larry Stellings–built Hemi-powered dragster. A month after its record run, the car was stolen at the Bakersfield March Meet. The local police combed the city of Bakersfield for the missing top fueler, and after an exhausting search, the car was found in a garage in downtown Bakersfield. Police returned the wayward fueler to Stellings and Hampshire just in time to race at the March Meet.

Tom McEwen was 15 years old when he "borrowed" his mom's car to go drag racing in 1950. Then in 1964, McEwen was driving the Donovan and Dawes top fuel dragster. He did very well in this car and beat up Prudhomme so much that Ed Donovan gave McEwen the nickname "the Mongoose" because the mongoose is one of the few animals that kill snakes one-on-one. Prudhomme was starting to use his nickname of "the Snake" so why not "Mongoose" for McEwen? The duo's rivalry became legendary in the history of the sport of drag racing. (Courtesy of the Greg Sharp Collection.)

One of the top-notch top fuel teams in Southern California in 1964 was the team of Bill Crossley, "Fat" Jack Williams, and Don Swan. Together, they won the 1964 NHRA Winternationals at Pomona, California. Then they won five out of seven NHRA Division 7 World Championship Series Races. Division 7 was the hardest to compete in because this is where all the SoCal top fuel cars raced for NHRA points. Driver "Fat" Jack Williams had a stellar year against some of the finest running fuel dragsters in the United States. It was a benchmark year for the team. (Courtesy of the Greg Sharp Collection.)

The 1960s top fuel dragster racing in Southern California was described by racers as the toughest in the country. To race in top fuel SoCal style, one had to be smarter and cleverer than their opponent, not richer, like the class became in the 1970s. The mid-1960s saw some great top fuel duels like Moody and Davis top fueler versus the Frantic Four top fueler. Hardnose, close racing, and putting on a show for the fans in the stands was drag racing during this era. (Photograph by Dave Shipman; courtesy of the Greg Sharp Collection.)

The Safford, Gaide, and Ratican team won 17 of the 22 races that they attended in 1963. Kenny Safford drove the nitro-burning Oldsmobile dragster to a February 2, 1964, win over the unbeatable Greer, Black, and Prudhomme top fuel dragster at Lions. The Oldsmobile-powered top fueler ran well but was extremely hard on parts. In one year of racing, the team went through 22 engine blocks. Tommy Ivo nicknamed the trio "the Sour Sisters" because of their demeanor after breaking so many engine parts. (Courtesy of the Greg Sharp Collection.)

The "Flyin' Hawaiian" Danny Ongais won top gas at the 1964 NHRA Winternationals in Pomona, California. Soon after that event, he went on top fuel racing with the team of Broussard, Davis, and Garrison and their Mangler top fuel dragster. Ongais and the Mangler set low ET at the Bakersfield March Meet in 1965 with a 7.60 ET. Later, in 1965, he ran the quickest and fastest ever for a top fuel dragster at Carlsbad, California. Then on April 25, 1965, he ran 7.55 ET at 207.36 miles per hour to claim that the Mangler was the quickest and fastest of all time. (Courtesy of the Greg Sharp Collection.)

Something different in Southern California top fuel for 1965 was the Scrima-Liner. The streamliner was the brainchild of race car and chassis builder Ronnie Scrima. Here, pictured with the almost finished car, are Don "Milodon" Alderson (standing left) and a kneeling Ronnie Scrima. The finished car would hit SoCal drag strips in mid-1965 with Roy "Goob" Tuller at the controls. The car was beautiful with its candy-red paint, but the car proved to be too heavy and was parked at the end of 1965. (Courtesy of the Greg Sharp Collection.)

Twenty-one-year-old Roland Leong came from Hawaii to Southern California to become a major player in the top fuel eliminator class. Roland wanted to be an owner/driver but after crashing his all-new "Hawaiian" top fueler at Lions, Keith Black advised Leong to give up driving. Black had another driver for Leong's Hawaiian fueler. Since Greer, Black, and Prudhomme disbanded, Prudhomme had no ride. Black put the two together, and they clicked, so now the Hawaiian had Don Prudhomme at the controls for 1965. The duo became a top fuel juggernaut, winning about every race they entered in 1965.

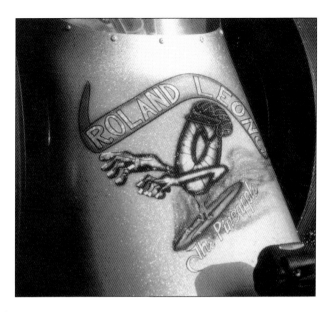

Don Prudhomme drove Roland Leong's the Hawaiian top fuel dragster to wins at the 1965 NHRA Winternationals in Pomona, California, and the 1965 NHRA US Nationals at Indianapolis. This was the first time this had ever been done by a top fuel team. But Roland and Company were not as lucky on the ride back to Southern California. They crashed the entire rig and damaged the race car. Leong and crew were not injured, but it took all the winnings from Indy to fix the bent race car. (Courtesy of the Greg Sharp Collection.)

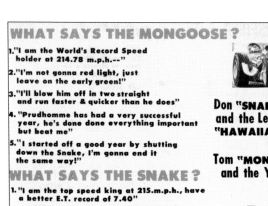
In the mid-1960s, Don Prudhomme and Tom McEwen took full advantage of their "Snake versus Mongoose" rivalry. SoCal top fuel fans flocked to see who would come out on top when they raced at Lions or any other track in the area. Prudhomme was at the wheel of Leong's Hawaiian while McEwen drove Lou "Wolfman" Baney's "Yeakel Plymouth Special." On this long-ago evening at Lions, the Mongoose was the victor over the Snake.

The Battle of the Southern California drivers at the "NorCal" Fremont Drag Strip saw "Wild Bill" Alexander in the local "Cheetah" top fuel dragster versus Dave Mackenzie driving his Mackenzie and Reath "Black Beauty" top fuel dragster. Mackenzie won this round, but Alexander set low ET for the day with a 7.54. Not only did Alexander drive a NorCal top fueler, but he still had rides back home in SoCal with the Beaver Bros. and their top fuel Chevy-powered fueler and the Brissette and Yates top fuel dragster. Never a dull moment for Alexander.

Another streamliner that tried to make waves in 1965 in Southern California belonged to Robert "Jocko" Johnson. His "Invader" was vastly different than other top fuelers of that time period. This was the second version of his streamliner, the first had a Chrysler Hemi. The second one (pictured) used an Allison Aircraft engine for power. The car was too heavy and never lived up to its potential. The first version debuted in 1958 (Hemi on nitro), and then seven years later, the Allison-powered car debuted with Emery Cook driving. Johnson's biggest claim to fame is that it was the first streamliner in SoCal top fuel class.

Frank Hedge brought A&W root beer in as the first soft drink sponsor into top fuel with his root beer–sponsored fueler in 1964. Hedge owned an A&W root beer fast food place in SoCal, so naturally, his car was sponsored by A&W. Walt Stevens drove the first root beer fueler in 1964, and then in 1966, Neil Leffler drove the car to runner-up at the Mickey Thompson 200-miles-per-hour club event at Lions. Bob Downey took over as the driver after Leffler in late 1966.

The first round at the 1965 *Hot Rod* magazine championships in Riverside, California, had Billy Scott driving the Scotty's Muffler Chevy top fuel dragster versus Don Prudhomme in the Hawaiian top fuel dragster. The 16-year-old Scott headed for the stars with his fueler as Prudhomme streaked toward the finish line. Scott was the youngest licensed top fuel driver in the country. He also drove the Beacon Auto Parts top gas dragster and at the 1967 NHRA Winternationals drove John Peters's top gas twin "the Freight Train." Scott left drag racing for oval track racing, and in 1976, he qualified for the Indianapolis 500.

It was the biggest win of his career when Nando Hasse won top fuel eliminator at the 1965 *Hot Rod* magazine championships in Riverside, California. Driving the Smyser and Hasse "Radar Wheels Special" fueler, he waded through a star-studded top fuel field that included the Hawaiian, Danny Ongais, the Frantic Four, "the Surfers," and Jim Dunn, just to name a few. Nando was a true underdog who got that victory bone on that long-ago weekend in Southern California.

TV Tommy Ivo started racing in 1957 with his custom T-Bucket street rod; he cranked out 12 seconds and 117-plus miles per hour out of T-Bucket. After his street rod, he built and raced a series of single- and dual-engine dragsters, then his four-engine "Showboat," and of course, his top fuel dragster, "the Barnstormer," in 1962. Then, in 1965, Ivo was trying his streamliner for top fuel racing. He debuted the car at Fremont's March championships. His "Video-Liner" proved to be very unstable at high speeds; with those results, Ivo sold the car and returned to the conventional front-engine top fuel dragster.

Mike Sorokin piloted the Skinner, Jobe, and Sorokin Surfers top fuel dragster as it put a massive hole shot on a very sleepy Denny Miliani driving Ted Gotell's NorCal-based fueler. Sorokin easily won that first round at the 1965 *Hot Rod* magazine championships, but the car had burned a piston with that win. In their haste to get back to their pit area to fix the engine, they ran the front of the race car into the back of Ed Pink's tow truck and destroyed the front end. There was no second round for the team—they were done for the weekend.

In the mid-to-late 1960s, Dave MacKenzie was a cornerstone in top fuel racing in SoCal. He drove the Reath and MacKenzie Black Beauty top fuel dragster at SoCal and NorCal top fuel events. When he stepped away from driving, his interest stayed in the top fuel dragster class. MacKenzie went to top fuel racing as an owner, giving young talent like Kelly Brown, Gary Cochran, and John Collins driving experience in his top fueler. Brown and Cochran did okay for MacKenzie, but John Collins crashed two of MacKenzie's top fuelers in 1969, forcing MacKenzie to quit racing in top fuel.

From 1963 to 1971, top fuel dragsters were the pinnacle of Southern California drag racing. The drivers were aggressive, fearless, and outspoken. All drivers wanted to be record holders, winners, and history makers. Nitromethane was the king of fuels for SoCal dragsters; top fuel racing in Southern California was tough and innovative. This was done by people who worked a regular job during the week. Only a few made their living touring a top fuel dragster around the United States.

December 1965 produced this shocking headline in the newspaper *Drag World*: Prudhomme was leaving the Hawaiian. Then, in 1966, Don Prudhomme signed a deal to drive for Bob Spar and his B&M Torque Master top fuel dragster. This left Leong with no driver for the 1966 racing season. The move to the B&M car would prove to be not so great, as Prudhomme struggled to win. To this day, it is a move that Prudhomme regrets making.

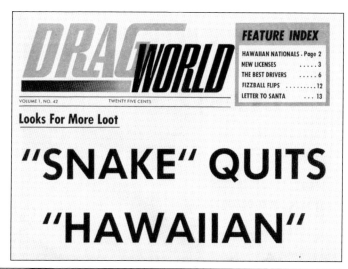

DRAG WORLD

VOLUME 1, NO. 42   TWENTY FIVE CENTS

Looks For More Loot

"SNAKE" QUITS "HAWAIIAN"

Bobby Tapia started driving dragsters right after high school in 1956. His first ride was the Tapia and Huffman dragster. The first top fuel car he drove was the Tarrant and Woodruff fueler. Then, in 1963, he got a ride in Don Prieto and Don Madden's top fuelers; 1964 saw him in John Harbart's "Pegasus" fueler. When Stellings and Hampshire broke up, Tapia became the new driver for Larry Stellings in 1965. The Stellings and Tapia top fuel dragster won the first-ever top fuel race at the Orange County International Raceway (OCIR) opener in 1967. Tapia drove for Stellings from 1965 to 1968 and then retired to work with computers.

In 1965, the team of Jim Ward and Jack Wayre raced two top fuel dragsters: one was the "Longshot," and the other was the "Shortshot." Ward drove one, and an Irish kid named John Mulligan from Garden Grove drove the other. Mulligan impressed Wayre with his natural driving style, and when Wayre teamed with Gene Adams in 1966, he named Mulligan as his driver.

Engine-builder Keith Black decided to have a garage sale at his South Gate, California, shop in 1965. After the Greer, Black, and Prudhomme team split up, Black ended up owning the once potent top fuel dragster. Black was tired of the car sitting in his shop so he simply placed a for sale advertisement in the classified section of NHRA's house newspaper, National Dragster. By selling the car, Black was able to recoup some of the money that had been owed to him by Tom Greer.

Nevada's Bill Butler answered Keith Black's advertisement, and a deal was made for the once-famous top fuel dragster. Butler redid the car with new paint, new lettering, and a new name: "Bonanza." Butler and his old/new fueler began racing in NorCal and the local Nevada drag strips. However, the car was hopelessly outdated and prone to "wheelstanding" because of its short wheelbase. Instead of chopping the car up and making it longer, Butler pulled the engine out of the car, and sans wheels and tires, he hung it in the rafters of his shop. From 1967 to the 1980s, the car hung in the shop until businessman and car collector Bruce Meyer purchased it from Butler's estate. Steve Davis restored the car to its glory days as the Greer, Black, and Prudhomme top fuel dragster. The car now resides in Meyer's car collection in Beverly Hills, California.

It did not take Roland Leong a long time to fill the seat of his Hawaiian top fuel dragster. Journeyman driver Mike Snively found a home for his driving skills with Leong's Hawaiian. Snively was no stranger to top fuel racing in SoCal or NorCal; he had driven Scotty's Muffler, Bill Martin's 400 Jr., and Ed Pink's top fuel dragster. In Ed Pink's car, he won the Northern California championships at Fremont in March 1965. Snively showed the SoCal top fuel world what he could do in a steady well-funded top fuel ride with Leong. That is Leong on the right and crew member Wes Hanson wiping down the tires on the Hawaiian just prior to making a run at Fremont in 1966.

Don Prudhomme had hoped that 1966 would be a banner year for Bob Spar's B&M Torque Master top fuel dragster. Unfortunately, that was not the case. His biggest win was at the Memorial Day weekend Olympics of drag racing in Rockford, Illinois. Prudhomme swept the event all three days. He ran the best of 7.53 ET at 218.19 miles per hour that long holiday weekend. The rest of 1966 was very bleak for the Snake. (Courtesy of the Geoff Stunkard/Quartermilestones collection.)

With the unsuccessful Video-Liner being sold, TV Tommy Ivo returned to his standard conventional full-bodied top fuel dragster. His wildly painted giraffe pattern turned a lot of heads and made the younger top fuel fans smile. Ivo, always the entertainer, knew how to get attention to himself and the top fuel class in 1966. He raced the giraffe car from 1966 through 1967 and was ranked third on the *Drag News* top-10 top fuel dragsters in the country.

Bob Skinner, Tom Jobe, and Mike Sorokin were known as the Surfers top fuel team. The trio was a ragtag race team out of Santa Monica, California. The base for the team and their car was Bob Skinner's mother's motel, the Red Apple Inn, in Santa Monica. The guys financed the car from a $7,000 furniture loan that Skinner's mom had secured from Bank of America. With that money, the Surfers went top fuel racing in a big way. Besides winning many a local SoCal top fuel race, they also won the 1966 Bakersfield March Meet. The winnings from the March Meet paid off their debt to Skinner's mom. Ironically, they never surfed a day in their lives. The trio just looked like SoCal surfer dudes and towed the race car with an old 1950s model Chevrolet. Once, they were asked, "What percentage of nitro do you run in the engine?" The answer was "100 percent of course because we kept breaking hydrometers."

SoCal and NorCal top fuel drivers often played musical driver's seats in 1966. SoCal's Kenny Safford (pictured) headed to the San Francisco Bay area to replace Roy Thode in the Gotelli Speed Shop top fuel dragster. Don Prudhomme took Safford's place in the Bob Spar-owned B&M Torque Master top fueler, and finally, Mike Snively replaced Don Prudhomme in Roland Leong's Hawaiian top fuel dragster—got all that?

Bobby "the Bat" Hightower scored his biggest top fuel win driving Dale Smart's "Vandal" top fuel dragster in 1966. Hightower won the AHRA (American Hot Rod Association) Winternationals at Irwindale, California. He made a single run in the top fuel final round because his opponent John Mulligan in the Adams and Wayre top fuel dragster had crashed on the "fire up" road while warming up a brand new just-installed engine for the final. Mulligan was not injured, and Hightower went home the victor. In 1967, Hightower changed rides when he went to drive Duane Trotter's top fuel dragster.

The sad saga of the Adams and Wayre top fuel team at the 1966 AHRA Winternationals would make grown men weep. Adams and Wayre were to race Bob Hightower in the final for top fuel eliminator honors. Unfortunately, they had hurt their engine in the semifinal round. Having enough time, they borrowed an engine from Oklahoma's Jimmy Nix and installed it into their race car. Driver John Mulligan jumped into the car, and it was pushed out onto the Irwindale fire up road to warm the new engine up. The car was pushed, and the engine came to life on the road. Mulligan hit the throttle, and the car made a violent turn off the road and rolled upside down, bending the chassis. Mulligan crawled out of the now upside-down car, and Bobby Hightower made a single for top fuel honors.

After the Surfers disbanded in mid-1966, Mike Sorokin drove for Ed Pink at the Mickey Thompson 200-mile-per-hour race at Lions. Then he could be found in Blake Hill's "the Grecian" top fueler (pictured) at the end of 1966. He got another top fuel ride in 1967 with Roland Leong's No. 2 Hawaiian top fuel dragster, but that only lasted a few months before Leong cut back to one race car in 1967. Next up in 1967 was a ride in Tony Waters's top fuel dragster. On December 30, 1967, at OCIR, a clutch explosion at speed in Waters's car took the life of Mike Sorokin. The entire drag racing community mourned the loss of one of their favorite sons.

After a hard weekend of racing at Half Moon Bay, California, in 1966, TV Tommy Ivo's top fuel dragster ended up on display in front of the Off-Broadway topless dancer club in South San Francisco. Miss Topless of 1966, Yvonne D'Angers, strolled out of the club to check out Ivo's race car. She gave her approval to Ivo's crew/ half-brother Don La Force before returning to the stage in the club. All this was done while Tommy Ivo was on an airplane going home to Burbank from the San Francisco Bay area. He knew nothing about the impromptu one-car show on the sidewalk in front of the club in South San Francisco.

THE
KILLER CARS
ARE COMING!!!
WHO? EVERYONE!
SMOKERS, INC. MARCH 4, 5, 6 and 7
WATCH THE WORLD's FASTEST DRAGSTERS "RACE" SIDE BY SIDE!!!
on
SATURDAY MARCH 6
STARTING AT 10:AM
TO GAIN POSITION FOR THE
TOP FUEL ELIMINATOR RUNOFF
PLACE: BAKERSFIELD!

It was the biggest and baddest top fuel dragster event in the United States and on the planet. The Bakersfield March Meet was the race every top fuel owner/driver dreamed about winning. Only the best of the best top fuel racers competed at this event. The race featured a 64-car first round of racing with 100-plus cars trying to qualify for those 64 spots. To win here is what dreams were made of for the top fuel racer. This race started in 1959 and is still going after 64-plus years. It may not have 64 cars now, but it does feature a great bunch of nostalgia top fuel racers trying to qualify for a 16-car field.

Two

ONLY THE STRONG SURVIVE

A top fuel dragster versus a jet-powered dragster here in December 1966, as John "the Black Knight" Edmunds driving Tony Waters's top fuel dragster matched up with J.D. Zink driving "the Untouchable" jet dragster. This combination of dragster versus jet was started by TV Tommy Ivo. Ivo, always the entertainer, saw how the drag fans reacted to jet cars at night so why not match race jets while on tour? With flames and smoke from both dragster and jet, it was a spectacular sight at night. Ivo nicknamed the jet dragsters "Weenie Roasters," and when he raced one, a long stick with a weenie would be sticking out of Ivo's car as it was pushed toward the starting line. The fans loved Ivo's showmanship and silliness toward his jet dragster opponents.

After a couple of successful seasons driving the Broussard, Davis, and Garrison Mangler top fueler, the Flyin' Hawaiian, Danny Ongais, left the team in 1966 to race on his own with his Honda of Wilmington top fueler. Ongais ran well, maybe too well, because at Irwindale, California, things went terribly wrong for the Flyin' Hawaiian. While entering the finish line at well over 200 miles per hour, the engine's crankshaft blew out through the bottom of the engine. The crankshaft dug into the track surface, and Ongais and his top fueler went end over end at 200 miles per hour. The car was destroyed, but Ongais walked away from the mangled race car. He returned at the beginning of 1967 with an all-new Honda of Wilmington top fuel dragster.

Mike Snively won the 1965 Northern California Championships at Fremont, California. He was driving for "the Old Master," Ed Pink, and his top fuel dragster. However, Pink changed drivers in mid-1965 as Florida's Connie Swingle took control of the sleek, pink-striped top fueler. Swingle did not disappoint Pink because he won one of the biggest top fuel races in Southern California in 1965; the first Mickey Thompson 200-miles-per-hour club race at Fontana, California. When Swingle left Pink in 1966, Mike Sorokin drove Pink's fueler at the second Mickey Thompson 200-miles-per-hour club event held at Lions. Because of so many business commitments and customers for his engines, Pink parked his top fuel dragster to serve his growing customer base across the United States.

Bill Holland and John Guedel's top fuel dragster rested on an RCS chassis with a Tom Hanna body and special custom paint by car show and customizer Bill Cushenberry. Ed Pink built a 392 Chrysler Hemi power plant that powered driver John Guedel to a record-setting 223.88 miles per hour at OCIR in 1967. Also, in 1967 at the opener for OCIR, they were runners-up to Bobby Tapia in top fuel with Tom "Mongoose" McEwen driving their car. The team reached the ultimate goal for any drag car when it graced the cover of the December 1967 *Drag Racing* magazine.

Throughout the 1960s and early 1970s, Wild Bill Alexander could be found behind the wheel of a top fuel dragster. In SoCal or NorCal, Alexander always had a top fueler to drive. In 1965, he was runner-up to Prudhomme and the Hawaiian at the NHRA Winternationals; his ride was the Brissette and Yates top fueler. Here in early 1967, he is at the controls of the Plueger Bros. and Alexander top fuel dragster. In this car, Alexander was a low ET qualifier (7.19 ET) at the 1967 Bakersfield March Meet, which featured almost 75 top fuel dragsters all trying for that No. 1 spot.

This is the view that most other top fuel owners/drivers got to see of Roland Leong's Hawaiian top fuel dragster in 1965, 1966, and 1967. In 1965, with Prudhomme driving, Leong won the NHRA Winternationals and the NHRA US Nationals. In 1966, with Snively driving, Leong won the NHRA Winternationals again, and in 1967, with Snively driving, Leong won Bakersfield and the *Hot Rod* magazine championships at Riverside. In this photograph, with Mike Sorokin driving the Hawaiian II, Leong also won the Las Vegas championships in 1967.

Another failed attempt in 1966 at a streamliner top fuel dragster was the Mooneyham, Jackson, Ferguson, and Faust "Jungle Four" top fueler. The car looked sleek and very cool but looking cool does not win races. Driver "Jungle" Larry Faust had his hands full when making runs in the fueler. At high speed, it proved to be unstable and "wandered" at the finish line so much that it destroyed the timing lights at Lions when testing. The car was too heavy and ill-handling, so it was parked. Fans can still see the car as it now resides at the Don Garlits Museum of Drag Racing in Ocala, Florida.

The pride of Garden Grove was the Beebe Bros., Tim and Dave. They parked their blown Bantam roadster and went to top fuel racing in 1966. Along with Lee Sixt, together the trio wreaked havoc in the Southern California top fuel wars. They proved to be the most consistent winners in the SoCal top fuel class and took home over $30,000 in prize money in 1966.

It was back to the standard top fuel dragster for the Jungle Four in 1967. The foursome had failed with their streamliner, and the team disbanded at the end of 1967. Gene Mooneyham returned to his native Louisiana and opened an engine-building business. He still raced in top fuel out of his Louisiana-based shop with Mike Martini driving his "Mooneyham and Sons" top fuel dragster. He was also involved in an early blown Chevrolet Camaro funny car, the "Car Shop Camaro."

This dynamic duo is Byron Blair (left) and Leroy "the Israeli Rocket" Goldstein (right); together, they won the 1967 AHRA Springnationals in Odessa, Texas. Goldstein drove the Blair, Goldstein, and Crower top fuel dragster to victory over a red-lighting Dave Beebe in the Beebe Bros. and Sixt top fuel dragster. Beebe had the low ET of the event at 6.94. Other achievements by Goldstein were that he held the unofficial gumball chewing record. He stuffed 86 gumballs into his mouth and chewed them, showing it was not a fluke. He then chewed 80 sticks of gum at one time. All this excitement happened at Bob Creitz's Oklahoma shop.

The team of Tony Waters and John "the Black Knight" Edmunds was the 1967 AHRA World Champion in top fuel. They also set the official NHRA speed record at 226.12 miles per hour. The event was on May 7, 1967, in Carlsbad, California. The duo split at the end of 1967 with Edmunds going on to drive for NorCal's Berry Bros. and Bill Crossley in SoCal. Mike Sorokin then filled the driver's seat in Waters's top fueler.

Sid Waterman's first engine shop was located behind a local topless dancer bar in Redondo Beach, California. Racers loved it; engines and adult entertainment all at one stop. Waterman over the span of seven or eight years had a thing for drivers with the first name of Ronnie. These were the drivers that drove Waterman's top fuel dragsters—Ronnie Martin; Ronnie Goodsell; and Ronnie Hampshire, who was the longest Ronnie that paired with Waterman. Besides building engines, Waterman was well known for his development of fuel systems for race cars. For anyone who needed advice or help at the races, Waterman was available.

Late in 1966, Roland Leong was offered 426 elephant Hemi engines for his Hawaiian top fuel dragster. This was made possible through Keith Black and Chrysler Corp. Two other well-known top fuel racers were also offered the elephant Hemi engine—"the Ramchargers" in the Midwest and Don Garlits in the East. Pictured is the Hawaiian II, driven by Mike Sorokin, in 1967, when Leong ran two Hawaiian top fuel dragsters. Sorokin went on to win the 1967 Las Vegas Open with Leong's No. 2 team top fueler before Roland went back to one car in top fuel in mid-1967.

The first time Gary Gabelich drove a dragster was in 1960. In 1963, Gabelich drove Bill Martin's 400 Jr. blown Chevy fueler to Lions Drag Strip for the first seven-second run. Between 1963 and 1966, Gabelich would sometimes drive four different cars at the same time during the same race. This practice was outlawed in 1966 with the one driver, one car rule per event. At the 1967 Bakersfield March Meet, Gabelich drove "the Purple Gang" top fueler of Rossi, Rapp, and Maldonado. This was one of many cars that "Daring" Gary drove in the 1960s. Gabelich picked up the nickname of "Daring" Gary when as a teenager, he jumped off the Parker Dam in Los Angeles and lived to talk about it.

The 1967 NHRA Winternationals featured an all-improved Don "the Beachcomer" Johnson top fuel dragster. Johnson and his driver Bob Muravez (Floyd Lippencott Jr.) had won the 1966 Las Vegas Open and the Mickey Thompson 200-miles-per-hour race at Lions, so Johnson spent a few dollars of his winnings on new body and paint for his top fuel dragster's debut in 1967.

Jim Busby owned "the Beach Boys" top fuel dragster and was based out of Newport Beach, California. Brad Pruett was the original driver for Busby. On the opening day of the new super SoCal drag strip OCIR, Pruett became confused while the car was being pushed up the fire up road. In his confusion, he crashed the car into the guardrail that protected the photographer's area. Busby repaired the car for future events, but "Surfer" Hank Westmoreland took over the driving chores. Sadly, Brad Pruett died in a work-related accident. Pruett had been a roofer and fell to his death while on the job. Busby continued to race until 1968, when he sold the top fueler to Dwight "Baby Huey" Salisbury.

La Mirada firefighter "Big" Jim Dunn wheeled "the Green Mountain Boys" top fuel dragster at Lions in 1967. This car was one of three cars built by Woody Gilmore that featured the trick "Praying Mantis" front suspension. Tommy Allen, McEwen, and Bivens raced the other two in 1967. One of these chassis ended up in Texas owned by the Anderson Bros. And driven by a young unknown driver named Kenny Bernstein in 1969.

Don "Snake" Prudhomme's new ride for 1967 was in Lou "Wolfman" Baney's Brand Motors Ford top fuel dragster. Ironically, the Snake replaced the Mongoose in the Wolfman's top fueler. The new team went to the Bakersfield March Meet and set the top speed for the event at 216.86 miles per hour. Then they towed to the 1967 NHRA Springnationals in Bristol, Tennessee, where they raced another Ford-powered top fueler for top eliminator honors. It was the first time two Ford-powered top fuelers raced in the final round. The Snake beat Georgia's "Sneaky" Pete Robinson in that final race with a 6.92 ET, 222.76 miles per hour to Robinson's losing 7.20 ET, 177 miles per hour. Later the same year, Prudhomme and Baney won the first Professional Dragsters Association (PDA) race at Lions, beating John Mulligan in the final.

It was late 1966 when the Surfers disbanded, and the car was sold to Jim Hoskinson sans their famous yellow injector scoop. The car was renamed "the Trip," with Walt Stevens as the driver. After a couple of ho-hum seasons, the car was sold to artist Tom Hunnicutt. Hunnicutt had no luck running the car with different engine combinations in it. He sold the car to a Midwest-based lawyer, and the lawyer quickly turned and sold the car. It then disappeared into the Midwest, never to be seen again.

Jim Brissette had quite a few drivers drive for him and his top fuel dragsters; Wild Bill Alexander, Don "Cement Head" Yates, Bob "Underdog" Noice, and Paul "the Kid" Sutherland to name a few. Sutherland won the 1965 AHRA National top fuel championship in the Brissette and Sutherland top fuel dragster. Home base for the team was Long Beach, California, just down the road from Lions Drag Strip.

It was May 1965 at Lions when "Big Daddy" Ed Roth made his first appearance with journeyman driver Connie Swingle doing the driving. Swingle made all the shakedown runs on a new top fueler, and then Roth's regular driver George "the Bushmaster" Schreiber took over. On July 23, 1965, the car caught fire when the fuel tank ruptured while racing in Carlsbad, California. Schreiber received burns on both of his wrists. The car was repaired and raced until late 1968–early 1969 and then was put on display at car shows. Fast forward to the present, and "the Yellow Fang" has been restored where it rests on display at the Don Garlits Museum of Drag Racing in Ocala, Florida.

Frank Pedregon started racing in 1958 in his native Texas. His first race car was an A/Comp coupe that ran 10 seconds and 130 miles per hour in the quarter-mile. By 1963, he had moved to SoCal and built his first 392 Chrysler Hemi for $35. His Hemi was built from broken or discarded parts from other racing cars. His homebuilt junk Hemi ran 8.93 at 173 miles per hour on gasoline. Pedregon then went top fuel racing with results that were not expected. A parachute failure at San Fernando destroyed the car, but thankfully, Pedregon was not injured in the crash. He began to regroup with the help of his godfather Bill Coburn as he put together his "Taco Taster" coupe. To run in top fuel, he took the body off the car and put it in his backyard, where it became a chicken coop.

"The Ol' Gray Fox" Jack Ewell had been racing dragsters since the 1950s. His greatest day of driving his Ardun powered dragster was on June 26, 1955, in Santa Ana, California. On that long-ago day, he beat Calvin Rice, Art Chrisman, and the Bean Bandits top fuelers to take home top fuel eliminator honors. Here, in 1967, Ewell and his crew pose for a group photograph at the 1967 NHRA Winternationals in Pomona, California. Ewell is at center with his trademark gray hair.

If the Surfers continued to race in 1967, this was the car that had been built for them. Instead, it was sold to the Bandel Bros. out of New York sans an engine. Bandel brother Richie drove it at the 1967 NHRA Winternationals in Pomona, California. Then the brothers packed up and headed back to New York. They were no strangers to running a top fuel dragster; they had purchased Garlits's "Swamp Rat VII," renamed it, and raced it as their "El Kabong" top fuel dragster.

The very brief partnership between Don "the Beachcomer" Johnson and Tom "Mongoose" McEwen produced a 6.97 ET at Carlsbad, California. The ET was good enough for a new national record in 1967. After they split later in 1967, McEwen went top fuel racing with Jerry Bivens, and Johnson teamed with "Surfer" Hank Westmoreland in top fuel.

Tommy "Watchdog" Allen drove the Huff and Allen top fuel dragster at 212.76 miles per hour on April 2, 1966, in Carlsbad, California. This miles per hour was good for a national record, but then on September 24, 1966, the San Diego–based team cranked out a 213.76 miles per hour at Irwindale, California. They reset their own NHRA miles-per-hour record set earlier in 1966. Huff and Allen utilized one of Woody Gilmore's trick Praying Mantis front ends on their top fueler.

A regular weekend warrior in SoCal top fuel racing was the Beaver Bros. top fuel dragster. This version of the car was driven by Hank Clark, and Gene Beaver tuned their 392 Chrysler Hemi. Beaver had a lengthy line of top fuel dragsters that raced in SoCal. He started with a blown nitro-burning Chevrolet-powered top fueler, which was sometimes driven by Wild Bill Alexander. When Beaver ran his car at local top fuel races, he would sometimes bring his teenage nephew. That wide-eyed teenager became funny car star John "Brute" Force.

Steve "the Mandrill" Carbone could be a bit of a show-off while driving the Beacon Auto Parts top gas dragster. Here, at Riverside, California, in 1967, he had a friendly wave to the photographers while on a banzai run. Carbone often did double duty at major SoCal events. He could also be found driving John Bateman's Atlas Oil Tool Special top fuel dragster at the same race.

Two of the biggest names in top fuel racing went head-to-head at the 1967 *Hot Rod* magazine championships in Riverside, California: Don "Snake" Prudhomme drove Lou "Wolfman" Baney's Brand Motors Ford (nearside) and was pitted against Mike Snively driving Roland Leong's Hawaiian No. 1 (far side). When the smoke cleared, the Hawaiian No. 1 took the win. Snively and Leong went on to win the top fuel eliminator that weekend.

Mike Snively started to get noticed when he drove Bill Martin's 400 Jr. and Scotty's Muffler top fuel dragsters. Snively drove the 400 Jr. to a top fuel speed record (for Chevy-powered dragsters) of 201.34 miles per hour at Fontana, California. While driving for Ed Pink, he was runner-up at the 1965 Bakersfield March Meet and won the Northern California Championships a week after Bakersfield. In 1966, Snively started off in the driver's seat for Roland Leong's Hawaiian top fuel dragster. Snively and Leong went on to win both the 1966 NHRA Winternationals and the NHRA US Nationals. Then 1967 dawned, and the duo was back winning races, including the Bakersfield March Meet, the *Hot Rod* magazine championships, and the Rockford 500 in Rockford, Illinois. They finished off 1967 by winning the Mr. USA Top Fuel Invitational on the East Coast. Here, Snively poses for a piston advertisement that was featured in *Drag News*.

Prior to 1968, the team of Wilton and Doss Bros. raced one of the quickest and fastest Chevy top fuel dragsters in the United States. Trying to keep up with the Hemi top fuel dragsters caused a lot of broken Chevy parts and engines for the team. In 1968, the team became the Doss Bros., and Bob Brooks switched to a 392 Hemi for power. Del Doss tuned the nitro-gulping Hemi, and Brooks was in the driver's seat. The team did not jell and broke up in late 1968. Doss put his Hemi into NorCal's Ed Carter and his "Proud American" Corvette funny car for 1969.

Bob Keough and Chris Eans owned the K&G Associates Speed Shop in Hagerstown, Pennsylvania. They purchased the entire Frantic Four team's top fuel dragster and rig in 1966. Jim Fox and Ron Rivero went with K&G, but Norm Weekly and Dennis Holding stayed on the West Coast. Fox continued to build engines and tune them while Ron Rivero was slated to do the driving of the top fueler. Then in 1968, Ron Rivero won the Bakersfield March Meet (pictured), and he was NASCAR top fuel champion in the bright-yellow Don Long–built top fuel dragster. The K&G owners purchased a never-run Mustang funny car from Phil Bonner in 1969 and ran both a funny car and a top fuel dragster. Rivero did double duty driving both race cars.

Jim Nicoll started 1967 with one top fuel dragster, and then in 1968, he expanded to a two-car team. The second car was driven by Nicoll's good friend Leroy "the Israeli Rocket" Goldstein, and both carried the "Der Wienerschnitzel" logo. Goldstein was runner-up to Ron Rivero at the Bakersfield March Meet in Nicoll's "Weinermobile" in 1968. The first Der Wienerschnitzel top fuel dragster, "Top Dog" or "Thunder Dog," was not even Nicoll's car. He had secured the sponsorship but had no car to race so a quick phone call to NorCal pal Don "Mad Dog" Cook, and the Der Wienerschnitzel logo adorned Cook's top fuel dragster until Nicoll's new car was ready to race. The first version of the Nicoll and Cook's Der Wienerschnitzel fueler appeared on the cover of the November 1967 issue of *Drag Racing* magazine. This made the Der Wienerschnitzel people incredibly happy.

"Little Dave" Babler owned and drove one of the first touring top fuel dragsters out of SoCal. His "California Woody" top fueler featured an RCS chassis with real wood strips down the sides of the car's body. Babler toured all over the United States and became a fan favorite in the Midwest and East Coast for over five years.

It was a matchup of SoCal versus Oklahoma at the 1967 NHRA Winternationals in Pomona, California—SoCal's Jerry Bivens driving the Bivens and Fisher top fueler (nearside) versus Tulsa's Gene Goleman in the Creitz, Greer, and Goleman top fueler (far side). The Oklahoma-based top fuel dragster raced on to the finish line, but Bivens had engine woes when his connecting rod came out of the engine and he had to shut off his fueler. Goleman went on to be runner-up to Connie Kalitta for top fuel eliminator honors at the event.

Was it a top fuel dragster or a long fuel-burning roadster disguised as a top fuel dragster? Lions Drag Strip was the only SoCal venue that had a class for these top fuel/long roadsters. They were basic top fuel dragsters but had a small cubic inch engine with either a Fiat, roadster, or T-bucket body mounted on the car. In this photograph is Larry Dixon Sr. driving the Fireside Inn T-bucket fueler, or as Lions classified them, "Double A" modified fuel roadsters. A few of the popular cars in this bracket were Frank Pedregon's Taco Taster coupe with a Fiat body, Eddie Potter's "Sudden Death" 1934 Ford coupe, Pete Millar's "Chicken Coop" 1934 Ford, Butters, and Gerard T-bucket and Jimmy Boyd's "Red Turkey" 1923 Ford pickup.

Fresno's Ed Wills traded his blown top fuel hydro drag boat for an asphalt top fuel dragster in 1968. Dan Olson was chosen to turn the wrenches and tune the blown Chrysler Hemi. Stan Shiroma took the driving chores as Wills raced in both NorCal and SoCal. Shiroma drove at first, followed by Oklahoma's Vic Brown, who took over in mid-1968.

To say top fuel dragster owner Steve Pick had bad luck with his top fuelers would be a vast understatement. On August 24, 1968, John Wilson, driving for Pick, was killed at Green Valley, Texas, during the AHRA Championships. Then John Martin borrowed Pick and Rupert's new car with an engine from Tom McEwen and attended the NHRA World Finals on October 19, 1968, in Tulsa, Oklahoma. Martin crashed and died in the borrowed top fueler. Tom McEwen came forward and bought Pick and Rupert a new car to replace the destroyed one. However, Pick was so distraught over Martin's death that he quit racing. The unused new car was sold to Carl Olson and Don Bowman.

The Caspary and Hampshire top fuel dragster was one of 20 top fuel dragsters that "Jumpin'" Jeep Hampshire drove in his top fuel career. This was his last top fuel dragster ride because on April 26, 1969, at OCIR he had a horrific crash in the car. Hampshire was on a great run when the car veered into the first guardrail at over 200 miles per hour, and it disintegrated upon impact with the second guardrail, leaving only Hampshire and the roll cage intact. Doctors saved his life that evening at the hospital, but his injuries prevented him from ever driving again.

The beginning of 1968 saw a new top fuel team: Tim Beebe and John "Zookeeper" Mulligan with their "Fighting Irish" top fuel dragster. Neither Beebe nor Mulligan were strangers to SoCal top fuel racing; Beebe raced with his brother Dave in top fuel, and Mulligan had driven for Ward and Wayre, the Beebe brothers, Adams, and Wayre from 1965 to 1967. They got noticed very quickly as they set the NHRA top-speed record at 229 miles per hour, the AHRA ET, and speed records at 6.66 at 226.50 miles per hour. After they toured in 1968, they held over 24 individual records across the United States. Not too bad for a couple of Irish boys from Garden Grove, California.

Bakersfield's hometown top fuel team of James Warren, Roger Coburn, and Marvin Miller scored big at the 1968 NHRA Winternationals in Pomona, California. The team known as "the Ridge Route Terrors" took home top fuel honors; this was their first major NHRA victory. They raced and won many local SoCal top fuel shows, but this was their biggest to date. The team came close in 1967 to winning the NHRA US Nationals but lost a close final round to Don Garlits. The most ironic thing about the loss was they had loaned a spare set of their slicks to Garlits for the final round.

Besides Joe Winter driving his own top fuel dragster, he had Ronnie Goodsell, Frank Pedregon, Harry Payne, and Kenny Logan all drive his race car at various times. Harry Payne drove Winter's "Swinger" top fuel dragster on August 14, 1965, to the winner's circle at the Palmdale Gold Cup Championships in Palmdale, California. Payne was not an ordinary guy driving a top fueler, he was a little different. He lived with 13 golden retrievers and once dove off a steamship in Long Beach harbor on a dare.

Roland Leong's swan song as a top fuel dragster owner was in 1968 with Stan Shiroma the last driver for him in top fuel competition. Then in 1969, Leong debuted a Dodge Charger funny car at the 1969 NHRA Winternationals with Larry Reyes doing the driving chores. Reyes flew and crashed Leong's funny car at its first-ever race. Leong rebuilt the car, and with Reyes still driving, he started to win races in SoCal and across the United States in 1969.

In the mid-to-late 1960s, SoCal drag fans loved the rivalry between the Snake and the Mongoose. Top fuel drivers started taking nicknames describing their personalities. Steve Carbone became "the Mandrill" (pictured), Tommy Allen went with "Watchdog," Bob Noice was "Underdog," Dwight Salisbury chose "Baby Huey," Bob Hightower was "the Bat," Jess Sturgeon was known as "the Flea," and Wayne King sharpened his talons because he was "the Peregrine." To keep all those animals and flying things at bay, Gerry Glenn was "the Hunter" and John Mulligan became "the Zookeeper."

Darryl Greenamyer was a Lockheed SR-71 test pilot and raced unlimited airplanes. He won his first-ever race in 1965 at the Reno air races. Greenamyer became a seven-time winner of the unlimited class, from 1965 to 1969 and in 1971 and 1972. His need for speed brought him to drag racing in 1967. Dave Zeuschel introduced him to the world of top fuel dragsters, and he was hooked. With his racing airplane sponsor Smirnoff Vodka, he went top fuel racing with Zeuschel engines, an SPE chassis, and a Bob Sorrell body. Both Greenamyer and Larry Dixon Sr. drove the beautiful top fueler from 1967 to 1969. The car graced the cover of *Drag Racing* magazine's October 1967 issue.

Dave McKenzie's Dean Engineering top fuel dragster was a regular at SoCal top fuel events in 1968. McKenzie had retired from driving so he let a few of the young aspiring drivers take the wheel of his top fuel dragster. Gary "Mr. C" Cochran (pictured) went from his top gas dragster to top fuel in McKenzie's car, and Kelly "the Controller" Brown was also given the opportunity to drive the car. It was Brown's first steady ride in a top fuel dragster. Cochran raced his own top fueler in 1969, and Brown found a home in Leland Kolb's car in 1969.

Wolfman, the Old Master, and the Snake had a banner year in top fuel racing in 1968. Don Prudhomme drove the Baney, Pink, and Prudhomme Ford-powered "Shelby's Super Snake" top fuel dragster to wins at the AHRA Winternationals, the NHRA Springnationals, the PDA race at Lions, and the Washington State Nationals and won the NHRA Division 7 World Championship Series (WCS) title. Ed Pink tuned the 427 Ford SOHC engine that rested in a Don Long–built chassis, and Baney supplied the cash to go racing.

Ronnie Goodsell's "Earthquake" top fuel dragster stood out among other SoCal top fuel dragsters. The Woody Gilmore chassis featured a trick front end with adjustable front-wheel suspension that had been developed on sprint cars. Goodsell's engine was built by Dallas Martensen and featured calliope-style injectors. Prior to having his own top fueler, Goodsell drove for Bob Sullivan, the Frantic Four, and Joe Winter.

George "the Stoneage Man" Hutchenson owned and drove his "Stoneage Man" top fuel dragster in SoCal around 1968–1969. The car featured an RCS chassis and Tom Hanna body. Hutchenson had recycled the former Mike Tingley "Mistrial" top fueler, and it became Hutchenson's Stoneage Man top fueler. In his spare time in 1968–1969, "Hutch" could be found behind the wheel of Don Green's "Rat Trap" fuel altered and Fling Traylor's "US Turbine" dragster. His ostrich-plumbed helmet became his trademark in SoCal top fuel racing.

Don Madden and Jerry Johanson combined forces and raced the Howard Cam Special top fueler. Here at Lions in 1968, Jess "Flea" Sturgeon made a smoke-filled pass in the top fueler. Other drivers that drove the car included "Daring" Gary Gabelich, Leland Kolb, Bobby Tapia, Neil Leffler, Roger Wolford, Don "Cement Head" Yates, Bob Downey, Norm Wilcox, Frank "Taco Taster" Pedregon, and Little Johnny Mitchell. In May 1965, Bob Downey drove the car to two big wins the same weekend at Lions, then Fontana the following day.

In the 1960s, Lions Drag Strip was the track to watch and race a top fuel dragster. The fans were so close that they could feel the cars zoom by the grandstands. Here, on a long-ago Saturday night in 1968, driver Denny Fitt launches the Fitt, Meyer, and Greth "Golden Boy" top fuel dragster to traverse down the Lions quarter-mile. Notice the special twin chute parachute pack that was first designed by Jim Deist for their car.

San Diego's Bob Williams came up through the dragster ranks, first in junior fuel car, then in top gas, and finally in a top fuel dragster. But in August 1969, his career and life almost ended on a highway outside of Salt Lake City, Utah. When Williams was returning to his hometown of San Diego after competing at the Division 7 WCS event at Bonneville Raceway, he and his towing rig were hit head-on. The horrific accident claimed the lives of Bob Williams's brother-in-law and the two people who struck his rig. Williams was severely injured, but he made a full recovery and raced the following year.

72

Irwindale raceway's Grand Prix of drag racing was a huge one-day event of drag racing in SoCal. At the 1969 Grand Prix, 42 top fuel dragsters attended to try and qualify for the 32-car field. This race also featured 16 junior fuelers and 16 funny cars all packed into one day of nonstop racing. When the smoke and nitro fumes cleared, Carl Olson, driving the Ewell, Bell, and Olson top fuel dragster, claimed top fuel honors over a stellar field of SoCal and NorCal top fuelers.

Once again, Larry Huff and Tommy "Watchdog" Allen joined forces in 1969 to go top fuel racing in the all-new "Soapy Sales" top fuel dragster. Their new fueler had the best of everything that Huff's money could buy. With Allen driving, the car toured the NHRA National event circuit and raced the Division 7 WCS circuit on the West Coast. A second Soapy Sales top fuel dragster was added to the mix toward the end of 1969 with Steve "Mandrill" Carbone driving.

Larry Dixon Sr. drove the "Howard Cam Rattler" top fuel dragster and won the 1969 *Hot Rod* magazine championships at Riverside, California. The final round of top fuel pitted Dixon against Steve "Mandrill" Carbone driving the Creitz and Donovan top fueler. It was a bizarre top fuel finish as Dixon smoked the Rattler's tires as Carbone hooked up and headed down the track for a sure win. Carbone's right arm was out of the speeding fueler with his hand signaling "V" for victory, while Dixon was trying in vain to get the Rattler to hook up its rear tires. Suddenly, Carbone's ride slowed down as it had broken the rear end; seeing this, Dixon mashed the throttle and passed Carbone to win top fuel eliminator.

Mike Kuhl and Bill Tidwell broke in a new top fuel dragster the wrong way at Lions in the late 1960s. In the final for top fuel honors, their top fueler dropped the crankshaft out of the bottom of the engine while entering the finish line timing lights. At over 200 miles per hour, the car erupted into a huge fireball and rolled down the guardrail, destroying itself. The accident earned Tidwell a hospital stay, and Kuhl brought out his wallet and built another car. Steve Carbone drove the replacement car until Tidwell returned a few weeks later.

The team of Beebe and Mulligan with their Fighting Irish top fuel dragster started out on a high note in 1969. They defeated Don Prudhomme in the top fuel final at the NHRA Winternationals to claim top fuel honors. It was their first big national event win, but sadly, it would be their last. At first things were going great at the NHRA US Nationals; they had run the low ET of the event 6.43 at 241.50 miles per hour for No. 1 qualifier. Monday, September 1 was the first round of eliminations; it paired them with Tommy Ivo. As their car entered the finish line ahead of Ivo, it exploded into a huge ball of fire. The car veered into the guardrail and destroyed itself, throwing driver John Mulligan out of the car. Mulligan suffered serve burns and injuries, and he clung to life for almost two weeks before succumbing to his injuries. Mulligan was only 26 years old. The drag racing community mourned the loss of one of its favorite sons.

Don Prudhomme's first dragster was a B/Gas dragster purchased from Tommy Ivo in 1961. Then in 1969, Prudhomme was on his own and purchased the last Hawaiian top fuel dragster from old friend Roland Leong with $7,000 in sponsorship money from Wynn's oil company. Engine credit was from another old friend, Keith Black, and the Snake was ready to race his old/new "Wynn's Winder" in top fuel.

Gary "Mr. C" Cochran left the world of top gas dragsters and his ride in Dave McKenzie's top fueler in late 1969. Cochran built his own top fuel dragster on a rather meager budget; he did almost everything himself on his new race car. His biggest win in his own car came in 1971 at Lions, when as a clear underdog, he defeated Don Garlits's new rear-engine top fueler in the final at the AHRA Grand American event.

From the mid-1960s to 1969, La Mirada firefighter Jim Dunn drove the Dunn and Reath top fuel dragster. The team was a true fixture in top fuel racing in SoCal and could be found racing every weekend at local drag strips competing with the best in SoCal. One of their biggest local wins was at the third annual Grand Prix of drag races at Irwindale when they beat the Hawaiian in the final. Dunn and Reath's other big top fuel win came at the 1969 Bakersfield March Meet. One hundred fifteen top fuel dragsters attended the event, and in the final round, Dunn outran Dave Babler for the top fuel crown.

TV Tommy Ivo's first year of touring the United States with his dragster was in 1960. He had a kid helper named Don Prudhomme, and Ivo paid the kid $25 plus expenses to tour. Prudhomme also drove Ivo's four-engine Showboat dragster too. Fast forward to 1969, and this was Ivo's touring rig; it contained two top fuel dragsters and a Chevrolet Corvette streetcar. Prudhomme had started to race and tour his Wynn's Winder top fuel dragster the same year.

The Bakersfield March Meet in 1969 played host to 115 top fuel dragsters that tried to qualify for one of 32 spots. One of those cars trying to make the cut was "the Vaporizer" driven by Little Dave Babler, a true veteran of SoCal top fuel racing and one of the first to go on tour across the United States. Babler barely made the field and was given no chance to even get out of the first-round eliminations. He was very much an underdog. However, drag racing is a sport not done on paper but on the racetrack, so when the final round came about, there was Babler and the Vaporizer racing Jim Dunn for all the gold. Babler was runner-up to Dunn that day but proved that no one should underestimate the underdog in top fuel racing.

Showing that a top fuel dragster is not for off-roading is San Diego's Bob "the Green Kid" Mayer. He received a face full of hot oil while driving his Speedmasters top fuel dragster at Sacramento in 1969. Mayer ventured into the wide-open spaces of the NorCal-based racetrack shutdown area. When the car finally came to rest, it was bent up badly, but Mayer was okay to fix his racer and race another day.

Joe Winter started racing in 1949 with a V-8-powered roadster. He built his first dragster featuring a blown Chrysler Hemi engine in 1962. Here at the 1969 NHRA Winternationals in Pomona, California, Winter drove his Swinger top fuel dragster. Prior to 1969, Winter did have other drivers behind the wheel of his top fuelers; they included Harry Payne, Ronnie Goodsell, Frank Pedregon, and finally, Kenny Logan. Winter was the only driver in top fuel who only had one leg, and he never let that stop him from driving. In 1971, he made the switch from top fuel to funny cars and drove it himself.

SoCal's Tommy Larkin was a little guy in the world of top fuel racing. Larkin and his wife, Margie, first raced a top gas dragster, but in 1969, he got the itch to go top fuel racing. Larkin did everything on his own, including building the blower on his Chrysler Hemi engine. Larkin built blowers for other top fuel and funny car racers and was remarkably busy with customers, which helped fund his top fueler. At times, when Larkin wanted to watch his car go down the racetrack and see how it was performing, he had Johnny Mitchell drive his top fueler. The Larkins took their race car to the track on an open trailer, which, one time, almost proved costly for them. Returning home after a race, Larkin noticed some wrong with the trailer—it was missing a complete blown Chrysler engine. He jumped in his wife's car and backtracked, and there was the engine two blocks from home, lying in the middle of the street.

Ronnie Goodsell's Earthquake and Jim Nicoll's Der Wienerschnitzel fuelers had two different approaches to top fuel dragsters while at OCIR in 1969. Goodsell's car was Woody Gilmore built with a trick sprint car type front end. Nicoll's Der Wienerschnitzel was built in Texas by Moose Schroeder at T-Bar Chassis. At the end of 1968, Nicoll cut back to just one Der Wienerschnitzel top fueler. Nicoll's biggest win in 1969 was at Cordova, Illinois, during their World Series of Drag Racing, which was a three-day event.

Tony Waters bounced back from the accident that took the life of his driver Mike Sorokin on the last day of 1967 at OCIR. Waters paired up with Wayne "the Peregrine" King for 1968, and then he went racing with Butch "C.W." Maas in the Waters and Maas top fuel dragster. In 1969, the duo competed in the NHRA division WCS and raced in NorCal and SoCal top fuel events. They also raced at a few AHRA and NHRA major races like the Grand American at Lions and NHRA US Nationals.

In May 1965, John Bateman was partners with Shingleton and Slusser in SoCal top fuel racing. Then in 1969, it was all Bateman with his Atlas Oil Tool Special top fuel dragster driven by Gerry "the Hunter" Glenn at Sacramento's El Dorado raceway. Bateman also had Pat Foster drive the sleek, beautiful, full-bodied fueler when Glenn was not available. Because of business commitments, the team rarely raced out of California. Bateman's last year in top fuel was in 1970, as he went funny car racing in 1971.

"Hand Grenade" Harry Hibler managed the San Fernando Raceway for over 10 years before getting the "need for speed." Hibler teamed up with John Smyser to race the Smyser and Hibler top fuel dragster. The team did okay at local SoCal top fuel events, with Hibler driving and Smyser tuning. Hibler and Smyser were runners-up to Tony Nancy at the 1970 Bakersfield March Meet in the top fuel eliminator. Hibler went on to drive for Marc Danekas, John Harbert, and Mike Butler, and if needed, Hibler also drove Don Green's Rat Trap fuel altered.

After leaving his ride in Jim Busby's Beach Boys top fuel dragster, "Surfer" Hank Westmoreland drove for Jim and Alison Lee in Plains, Virginia. Then in 1969, Westmoreland returned to SoCal and drove for Don "the Beachcomer" Johnson and his top fuel dragster. "Surfer" Hank rode the big wave in 1969 when he won the 1969 NHRA Springnationals in Dallas, Texas. It was an all-SoCal final as Westmoreland defeated Kelly Brown in Leland Kolb's top fuel dragster for top honors.

Tom "Mongoose" McEwen debuted his all-new top fuel dragster at the 1969 NHRA Winternationals in Pomona, California. This made it over 20 dragsters that the Mongoose had driven since he started racing in the dragster classes. Then in 1969, McEwen purchased a low-mileage funny car from Candies and Hughes. McEwen decided to race in top fuel and funny car classes for 1969, and Team Mongoose became a double threat at national events across the United States.

Lou "Wolfman" Baney played musical drivers in 1969. His Shelby's Super Snake top fuel dragster featured a Ford SOHC 427 for power until Ford pulled out of racing at the end of 1969. The car also had a name/sponsorship change to Foulger Ford, and a Chrysler Hemi replaced the Ford engine. Driving for the Wolfman was either Kelly "the Controller" Brown or Bill Tidwell (pictured).

Chuck Griffith's "Starlite III" top fuel dragster was a basic example of an early Kent Fuller–built top fueler. The car was beautiful but very outdated in 1969. Griffith ran a Ford SOHC 427 engine until Ford pulled out of racing late in 1969. He replaced it with a 392 Chrysler Hemi built in 1957 but never updated the car's chassis. The car did feature a beautiful paint job and a body by craftsman Arnie Roberts.

Dwight "Baby Huey" Salisbury purchased the Beach Boys top fueler from Jim Busby in 1969 and got serious about racing in top fuel. Salisbury raced the car through the 1970 season, and he picked up the comedy team of Tom and Dick Smothers as cosponsors of the fueler. When the 1970 season of racing started, it was Salisbury's fifth year of racing either in top fuel or top gas.

The San Diego–based team of Leonard Abbott and Joe Lee raced "the Shifter" top fuel dragster in SoCal. The car was considered a rolling lab for the racing transmissions that were being marketed by Leonard Abbott. Joe Lee did the driving of the top fueler until he went funny car racing. Then the car was sold to Ted Cyr and Flip Schofield. Abbott's family had lost a family member to a drag racing accident on July 19, 1958. On that day, Norris Abbott, Leonard's brother, died at Paradise Mesa drag strip in San Diego.

Another SoCal top fuel driver that headed to NorCal was Bob "the Bat" Hightower. He did not race SoCal's top fuel cars but instead went racing with South San Francisco's Jessie Perkins and his "Cow Palace Shell" top fuel dragster. Hightower kept his funny car ride in SoCal; he was driver of Doug Thorley's rear-engine AMC bodied "Javelin" funny car until it flew and crashed at Irwindale. Hightower was not injured in the spectacular crash at the Irwindale finish line.

Southern California invaders scored big at the 1969 Sacramento Governor's Cup Championships. The top gas winner was Jack Jones (kneeling on the left), and the top fuel winner was Kelly "the Controller" Brown (kneeling on the right). Jones was driving the Schultz and Jones top gas dragster, and Kelly Brown was driving for the Leland Kolb dragster in top fuel. That is Kolb peeking over Miss Roddy's right shoulder.

The Mule Train top fuel dragster was one of many that journeyman Tom Ferraro drove in SoCal. Ferraro was mainly a driver of fuel altereds, but here in 1969, he drove the Mule Train fueler. In the decade of the 1970s, Ferraro changed rides to the funny car class, where he drove "the California Charger" Pinto, Rat Trap, and John Hovan's Mustang funny cars. All the while he still drove many different fuel altereds in that era.

Most SoCal top fuel dragster fans have never heard of Arnold and Charlie Parigian's "the Armenian" top fuel dragster. Back in 1964 and 1967, the "Armenian 1" (1964) and the "Armenian 2" (1967) raced at Fresno Dragway's four-wide top fuel event; it was the first of its kind in California. Yes, four top fuel dragsters racing side by side by side by side for the entire quarter mile. The 1967 event was the last time it was ever run in California. At the 1967 race, the "Lizard," the Armenian 2, the Berry Bros. and Stark, and Gotelli and Safford were the participants in the four wide. The Armenian 2 (pictured) had either Dwight Salisbury, Jack Martin, or co-owner Arnold Parigian driving.

Kelly "the Controller" Brown's first top fuel ride was tire testing Jim Brissette's top fuel dragster in 1968, and he also drove a top gas car. Next was a semipermanent ride in Dave McKenzie's top fuel dragster. In 1969, Brown was offered the ride in Leland Kolb's top fuel dragster; the team jelled, and Brown won nine out of 11 final rounds with Kolb's fueler. Brown and Kolb were runners-up at the 1969 NHRA Springnationals in Dallas, Texas. Another big runner-up was at the 1969 NHRA US Nationals at Indy. Brown's real job was being a Hollywood stunt driver, so this did limit his traveling to races. In 1970, when Kolb's car was parked, Brown drove for Lou "Wolfman" Baney and his "Foulger Ford" top fuel dragster.

Three

NOTHING STAYS THE SAME

Danny "the Flyin' Hawaiian" Ongais left his Mickey Thompson funny car ride at the beginning of 1970 and went top fuel racing. Car show guru Carl Casper offered Ongais a ride in his all-new "Young American" top fuel dragster, and Ongais jumped at the offer. Casper was based out of Louisville, Kentucky. However, the car was based out of Keith Black's shop in South Gate. This was not the first time Casper went top fuel racing; he owned "the Galloping Ghost" top fuel dragster that was driven by Butch Bryant in 1969. Ongais only drove the 1970 season for Casper, and in 1971, Gary Cochran filled the driver's seat. Cochran started 1971 off by winning the top fuel eliminator at the AHRA Winternationals in Scottsdale, Arizona.

Larry and Pat Dixon won their first-ever major NHRA event with a top fuel victory at the 1970 NHRA Winternationals in Pomona, California. The husband-and-wife team defeated their good friend Tony Nancy to claim that win at Pomona. A four-year-old Larry Dixon Jr. joined his parents in the winner's circle that day. Twenty-eight years later, Larry Dixon Jr. won top fuel at the 1998 NHRA Winternationals driving for Don Prudhomme and his "Miller Lite" top fuel dragster.

Tony Nancy's first real race car was a 1929 Ford roadster with a blown Ford flathead engine on nitro in the late 1950s. His line of 22 junior top gas dragsters was well-known in SoCal in the early to mid-1960s. Nancy's good friend Don Prudhomme convinced Nancy to go top fuel racing in 1969, so he made the giant leap from top gas to top fuel. It took Nancy about a year before he won his first big top fuel race, the 1970 Bakersfield March Meet. At that event, he beat lifelong friend Harry Hibler in the final round to claim top fuel eliminator. Nancy's win at Bakersfield was the last time a front-engine top fuel dragster would win top honors until Bakersfield hosted nostalgia top fuelers in the 1990s.

When jet engine mechanic John Keeling and airline pilot Jerry Clayton went top fuel racing in the late 1960s, they did it in style. Their California Charger top fuel dragster was a true show-and-go race car. The car featured the best parts and pieces that were available at the time. In the driver's seat was top gas standout Norm Wilcox, who only drove for a brief time. Another top gas standout, Rick Ramsey, filled the vacant driver's seat when Wilcox left the car.

The whole top of Jim Brissette's top fuel engine departed in a split second just after this photograph at OCIR in 1970. Driver Bob "Underdog" Noice received a face full of fire, oil, and pieces in the finish-line explosion. Noice rode it out and got the blower-less top fueler stopped safely. He suffered some minor burns, and the duo regrouped and went top fuel racing the following weekend. Just another weekend of SoCal top fuel racing.

This happy group is in the winner's circle at the NHRA WCS race at Bakersfield in 1970. The Schultz and Glenn gang saw quite a few winner's circles in SoCal. The team raced in both top fuel and top gas with Gerry "the Hunter" Glenn doing double driving duty. Bill Schultz built and tuned both the top gas and top fuel dragsters. Glenn is by the roll cage (second from right), and Schultz is in the middle with glasses.

Don Moody started driving in top fuel in 1962. In 1963, he teamed with Dave Zeuschel and Kent Fuller to race in SoCal's top fuel wars. On August 8, 1963, Moody crashed at Lions, and the car exploded upon impact with the end sign at the finish line. The only thing left was Moody strapped in the roll cage. Moody walked away from the crash. The other top fuel racers who witnessed the accident called it "The miracle on 223rd Street" (Lions's mailing address). Moody retired from racing and went back to his job managing Engle cams. Six years later, his good friend Wes Cerny coaxed him to come out of retirement to drive the Cerny, Lins, and Moody top fuel dragster (pictured).

Top gas and top fuel veteran Gene Adams tried something different in top fuel in 1970. He and his good friend John Rassmussen assembled a twin-engine injected top fuel dragster. The car used two injected nitro-burning 354 Chrysler Hemis for power nestled in a 225-inch Don Long chassis. The car had a Tom Hanna shorty body with a Cerny paint job; Don Enriquez was doing the driving. Adams's "Double Eagle" was on the cover of the August 1970 issue of *Drag Racing* magazine and its best was 6.74 ET at 217 miles per hour.

Toward the end of the 1960s and the start of the 1970s, a new dangerous burnout style was taking place in the top fuel dragster class. The fire burnout was very spectacular if done correctly or extremely dangerous if done wrong. One day toward the end of 1970 at OCIR, Kuhl and Tidwell burned one down for photographer Steve Reyes. The rear tires were splashed with a gallon of hi-test gasoline and ignited by the car's hot headers. Tidwell drove the car out of the huge fireball, Reyes got his photograph, and Kuhl and Tidwell got a cover on *Popular Hot Rodding* and a nationwide poster. The damage was as follows: a hole melted in the OCIR burnout box, the race car's paint destroyed, and the parachute pack burned off the car.

Blower failures were common in SoCal top fuel racing, as engine builders ran their engines on the edge of destruction each run down the quarter-mile. Here at Lions, the Schultz and Glenn top fuel dragster had a big blower boom. Pieces from the blower were a danger to the driver and spectators. Driver Gerry "the Hunter" Glenn escaped injury from the split blower casing and flying blower impellers that rained down on him.

Steve "Mandrill" Carbone had a few new car bugs to work out of his all-new top fuel dragster in late 1970. This was Carbone's first solely owned top fueler, and it proved to be a winner for him. His biggest win was at the 1971 NHRA US Nationals at Indianapolis. At that race, he beat Don Garlits's new rear-engine top fueler in the final. The pair engaged in a two-minute staging duel. Garlits went up in smoke, and Carbone sped to victory. Carbone's slingshot-style dragster was the last front-engine fueler to win at Indy. The 17-year-old slingshot design was now becoming obsolete.

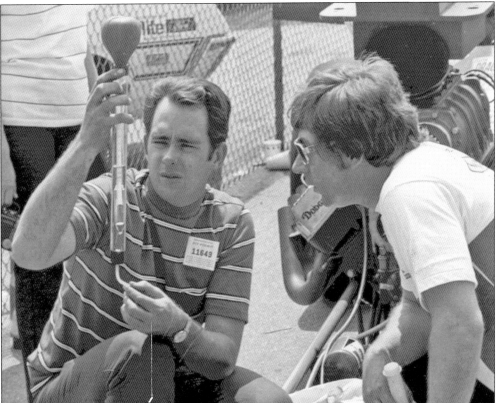

In 1952, SoCal racers adopted nitromethane as their "official" racing fuel. In 1970, Dwight "Baby Huey" Salisbury (left) and Bill Holland (right) used a nitro hydrometer to measure the percentage of their nitro and alcohol mixture. In 1929, Italian rocket scientists developed nitromethane, and the following year, Russian scientists tested a combination of nitro and kerosene derivative. In 1947, John Cobb ran 403 miles per hour in his land speed car on a mild batch of nitromethane. Ban or no ban, nitro was here to stay in SoCal drag racing.

Slowing down in the Lions Drag Strip shutdown area are Mike Clancy in the Butters and Gerard top fuel dragster (left) and Les Allen in the Allen family Praying Mantis top fuel dragster (right). To be honest, Lions looked like a dump during daylight hours. Then when the sun went down, it came alive with the sounds and smells of top fuel racing. From 1955 to 1972, Lions was the place to race a top fuel dragster. Every top fuel racer strived to win there; many tried but only a few could say that they won top fuel eliminator at "the Beach."

Mike and Bill Demerest raced in both top fuel and the fuel altered class. Their "Ground Shaker Sr." ran in top fuel, and the "Ground Shaker Jr." raced in fuel altered class. Their top fuel dragster was a regular at SoCal top fuel events and was driven by Gary Read. The fuel altered was a regular at SoCal fuel altered events with Glen Way driving. If Glen Way could not drive, then Gary Read stepped in to drive the altered. Read also drove in the "Nutcracker" AMC Javelin-bodied funny car and the "Mother-in-Law" fuel altered in his spare time.

The saga of the "Gold Seeker" top fuel dragster is a rather strange one. The car was first sold by Ed Pink to a group of Texas top fuel racers, and it became the "Lucky Dodge" top fuel dragster. Then their check bounced. So Pink repossessed the car and sold it to Larry Huff, and it became the Soapy Sales No. 2 top fueler. Then Huff sold the car to Joe Winter, and he and Kenny Logan ran the car for a brief time in late 1970. Then Winter sold it to an unknown party who named it the Gold Seeker and had NorCal's Dave Uyehara drive it. At the time, Uyehara was also driving Max Williams's "Instant Karma" top fuel dragster in NorCal.

When the team of Kuhl and Tidwell broke up, it did not take long for Kuhl to fill the driver's seat. Michigan's Dick Rosburg filled the cockpit in Kuhl's top fuel dragster for a brief period. Rosburg left Kuhl and returned to Michigan where he drove Tim Arnold's new rear-engine top fuel dragster. Again, in mid-1971, Kuhl needed a driver for his top fuel dragster. Meanwhile, Rosburg left top fuel and went funny car racing in the Fighting Irish Pontiac Firebird–bodied funny car that was based in Michigan.

Bob Ivett began 1970 as a newcomer in SoCal top fuel racing. He piloted the "Corr Electric" top fuel dragster at local top fuel races, and he also attended the 1970 NHRA US Nationals at Indianapolis. Ivett was one of a few SoCal top fuel racers who switched to the rear-engine design in the early 1970s. Many SoCal top fuel racers quit racing, as the SoCal drag strips began to close in the 1970s and they had to tow long distances to race.

Coming from the San Diego area to race was the trio of Sterling, Prock, and Brown. They mainly raced in SoCal and Arizona. They would make the transition from front-engine to rear-engine top fuel as they purchased Leland Kolb's "Polish Lotus" and removed the rear portion of the car's body to make it lighter. Frank Prock drove their new/old top fuel dragster for the trio.

This was the final round of top fuel eliminator at the 1970 NHRA US Nationals in Indianapolis. It was Don Prudhomme (nearside) versus Jim Nicoll (far side). Prudhomme would win by inches over Nicoll, but the aftermath of the race was scary. Nicoll's car had a clutch failure, which blew the car in half, sending pieces and parts of his car all over the shutdown area. The roll cage with Nicoll strapped in it tumbled over the guardrail into the grass. Meanwhile, farther down the shutdown area, Prudhomme waited to hear if his good friend had died in the explosion. Rescue workers got to Nicoll and cut him out of the roll cage, and then he calmly strolled over to the waiting ambulance to the cheers of the crowd. That was the day Nicoll earned his nickname "Superman."

The two titans of top fuel squared off at Fremont, California. In 1970, Florida's "Big Daddy" Don Garlits versus SoCal's Don "the Snake" Prudhomme. These two had been a feature match race in the San Francisco Bay area since 1966; Half Moon Bay was the track used from 1966 to 1969. Since the track was too short for the speeds that top fuelers were attaining, the match was moved to Fremont. Prudhomme sent Garlits home with two out of three wins. Prudhomme then started concentrating on funny car racing, and this was the last time they matched race in NorCal.

SoCal top fuel racer Norm Ries shows how not to do a fire burnout at Irwindale, California. In 1970, a Ries crew member poured the very flammable VHT traction compound on the hot headers, which caused it to ignite the whole bleach box. Note the bottle is on fire and so is his crew member's pant leg. Ries did not panic and drove out of the burning bleach box. He was incredibly lucky because if he had waited too long, the fire would have sucked the oxygen out of the air around the engine causing the car to stall in the fire.

When SoCal's "Rocket" Rod Dunne went top fuel racing, he did it in style with sponsorship from Dick Clark's television show *American Bandstand* in 1970. Since the television show had relocated from Philadelphia six years earlier to Los Angeles, this made it possible for Dunne, along with Tony Nancy, to appear on Clark's television show. When the rear-engine top fuel dragsters took over in top fuel, Dunne went racing with Larry Dixon Sr. Together, they raced one of the quickest and fastest Chevrolet-powered top fuel dragsters in the United States. After that, Dunne went rocket car racing and toured America.

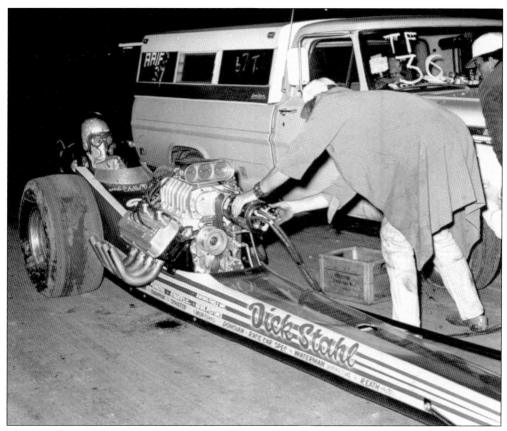

The giant human being starting his top fuel dragster is seven-foot-tall Dick Stahl. He was one of the more colorful top fuel owners in SoCal. Stahl had been married seven or eight times and was heir to the Chicken Delight fast-food empire based in Southern California. He started nitro racing with a blown Ford-powered roadster but then got the urge to go really fast, so he moved on to top fuel. Stahl had Walt Stevens, John Wilson, and Tom Tolar as drivers of his top fueler. Stahl made the switch to a rear-engine car in 1972 with Tolar driving and crew-member photographer Tim Marshall joined them; they toured the United States and Canada.

In 1958, Evert "Hippo" Brammer was a Southern California dry lakes racer. His dry lakes roadster ran its best speed at 212.26 miles per hour on the wide-open spaces of the dry lakes. Now, 12 years later, Hippo is going asphalt racing with money man John Pointdexter and driver Johnny Mitchell. Because of job commitments, Brammer's top fueler raced mainly in SoCal or a few side trips to Nevada for the Las Vegas Open. His driver Johnny Mitchell was no newcomer. Mitchell had driven a considerable number of top fuel dragsters before Hippo's top fueler.

After being retired for almost four years, Stormin' Norman Weekly returned to top fuel in Ted Gotelli's NorCal-based top fuel dragster in 1970. This was not just any top fueler, it had been five years since his good friend Denny Miliani died in Gotelli's top fuel dragster at Half Moon Bay. Miliani's death was the main reason Weekly walked away from drag racing. Norman only drove for a brief time in Gotelli's car and would be replaced by Norm Wilcox.

This is Don Green's Rat Trap fuel altered roadster and a relaxing ride for George "the Stoneage Man" Hutchenson when Hutch's top fuel dragster was parked. "Hand Grenade" Harry Hibler and Ron Boswell also had seat time in the Rat Trap. Green stayed with the fuel altered class until 1972 and then went funny car racing.

One of those little local guys in SoCal top fuel was swimming pool contractor Jack Raitt. In the mid-1960s, he owned the "Syndicate" top fuel dragster that was driven by Glen Woosley. During 1966 and 1967, the team was a semi-regular at top fuel events in SoCal. Business commitments and financial restraints kept them from running every weekend. Raitt had to race his car on an extremely limited budget.

John Guedel and Bill Holland's top fuel dragster was housed in their shop right off Van Nuys Boulevard in the San Fernando Valley in 1970. Race fans came by to bench race and check out their top fueler daily. On this day, a lovely lady named Lois happened to check out the race car. She worked on Van Nuys Boulevard as a nude dancer at one of the many dance clubs on the boulevard. Lois posed with the car in her bathing suit and some au natural, much to the delight of Guedel and Holland.

From 1955 to 1972, Lions Drag Strip was the premiere place to race a top fuel dragster in Southern California. The fans were rabid over top fuel racing and for major top fuel events; it was standing room only and sellout crowds for top fuel events at Lions. A good example was the July 1967 PDA race when 16,000 fans packed Lions to see the best of the best top fuel dragsters. That race was even covered in *Newsweek* magazine, which was a first for the sport of drag racing. The average top fuel show at Lions would draw 40-plus cars trying to qualify for eight or sixteen spots to race in eliminations. The racing was tough, but it was even tough just to qualify.

"The Israeli Rocket" Leroy Goldstein left his SoCal top fuel ride with Jim Nicoll and headed to Michigan for the cockpit of the Ramchargers top fuel dragster. Goldstein was now driving for one of the powerhouse teams in top fuel in 1969. Goldstein did very well in his first year as their driver by winning the 1969 AHRA Winternationals in Scottsdale, Arizona, and the 1969 Springnationals at Bristol, Tennessee. At Bristol, he beat Don Prudhomme in the final round.

Leroy Goldstein's last pass in the Ramchargers top fuel dragster was in 1969, and it was spectacular. At a Southwest racetrack, he blew the entire top off the engine in a huge ball of fire. Pictured are the burns he received in the fire, and they healed nicely. The Ramchargers ran the top fueler one more time with Jim Nicoll sitting in for the wounded Goldstein. The dragster gave way to a funny car as the Ramchargers went funny car racing in 1970 with Leroy Goldstein as the driver.

In 1970, the Dyer and Van Luven top fuel dragster with Norm Wilcox driving set a low ET at 6.75 at the 1970 Bakersfield March Meet. In this photograph taken in 1971, the car had been recycled as the "Ground Zero" top fuel dragster owned by Bob Magness and driven by John Walton. The car was hopelessly outdated and soon disappeared from the SoCal top fuel scene. Top fuel racers recycled in SoCal, and that gave newcomers a chance to see if top fuel racing was what they really wanted to do.

Upon selling his former Smothers Brothers–sponsored Beach Boys top fuel dragster, Dwight "Baby Huey" Salisbury had no problem securing a top fuel ride for 1970. The Ohio-based Drespling Bros. hired Salisbury to shoe their top fuel dragster at California top fuel events. When that ride finished for Salisbury, he drove the Korody/Colyer Corp. top fuel dragster at the end of 1970 and the beginning of 1971. Salisbury did build a rear-engine top fuel dragster in 1971.

The Butters and Gerard top fuel dragster driven by Mike Clancy (far side) squared off with an unknown top fuel dragster at OCIR. The unknown top fueler did not finish this run because the connecting rods are poking out of the oil pan. The Hawaiian top fuel dragster owner Roland Leong and other SoCal top fuel racers agree that SoCal top fuel racing was the most competitive in the country. To win in top fuel in SoCal meant top fuel racers ran their car's engine on kill each time they ran down the track.

Most SoCal top fuel owners only had one engine per event. But as competition got tighter and the stakes got bigger, more parts were used. Utilizing more than one engine per race became the norm for top fuel teams. Top fuel pit areas looked like war zones with frantic engine rebuilding or complete engine swapping to race in the next round of top fuel racing.

SoCal's Jim Hume tried something different in top fuel racing in 1971. He built a combination funny car and dragster-style chassis to run in top fuel. Hume sat upright in this rather strange-looking chassis design. Alas, Hume's one-of-a-kind top fuel dragster experiment produced a very evil-handling top fuel car. The car also utilized rear suspension, which did not help with the control issues. Hume tried for one season to make it work but then parked the car.

When his brother Jeep retired after his horrific crash at OCIR, Ronnie Hampshire continued racing in top fuel. A few of Hampshire's top fuel rides included the Waterman and Hampshire fueler; Caspary, Robinson, and Hampshire fueler; and in NorCal, a short stint in Ted Gotelli's top fueler. Hampshire did not make the transition to a rear-engine top fuel dragster; instead, he retired and continued his craft as a carpenter.

Top fuel dragsters came from all over the United States with one goal: to win top fuel eliminator at OCIR, Lions, or Irwindale. To win at SoCal was the ultimate achievement for an out-of-state top fuel team. In 1970, St. Louis–based banker Bruce Dodds and his "Spirit" top fuel dragster, with Bob Murray driving, tried his luck against the Waterman and Hampshire top fuel dragster driven by Ronnie Hampshire. Hampshire sent Dodds and Murray home to St. Louis empty-handed.

Pat Johnson's "Moonlighter" top fuel dragster was a semi-regular at SoCal and NorCal top fuel events in the late 1960s. Most of the time, former Washington state resident Frank Rupert drove for Johnson, but Hank Clark drove for him as well. Johnson parked his top fueler in early 1970 to go funny car racing with Hank Clark. Together, they raced the Chapman Automotive Camaro funny car that was based in Chicago. The third time out for the duo, they won funny car eliminator at the 1970 Bakersfield March Meet.

John Collins readied to go racing in Dave McKenzie's "Blue Streak Special" top fuel dragster at Irwindale in 1969. This is the last run on the car because Collins received a hot oil bath at the finish line and veered off the track and into a group of large rocks, which destroyed the car. Collins walked away, but that was the second car of McKenzie's that Collins had crashed; the first was at Lions when it blew over at mid-track. The crash put Dave McKenzie out of top fuel racing for good.

Formerly the R&R Engines top fuel dragster raced by Rocky Childs, "the Addict" top fuel dragster was the aftermath of an accident at Lions. Childs's R&R fueler was destroyed in a freak fire-up accident; the car crashed in the upper build-up area behind the starting line. It was very cold that evening at Lions, and the car failed to fire when pushed toward the starting line. Unable to stop, it crashed into one of the gates that blocked the upper staging lanes. Driver Walt Stevens was not injured, and the car returned as the "Childs and Albert Addict" top fuel dragster with Tom Tolar driving.

Ontario Motor Speedway opened in the latter part of 1970, and the first drag race held there was the NHRA Supernationals. Former top gas standout Roger "Ramjet" Gates had the honor of having the first big top fuel dragster fire with his "Cracklin' Rose" top fuel dragster in Ontario. Gates escaped with minor burns as the fire burned the chute pack and burned the paint off the car. Gates returned to top fuel for a while, but he parked his top fueler and went racing on the Bonneville Salt Flats, his first love.

To say "Blazin'" Gary Hazen liked nitro racing would be a vast understatement. In a span of four years, from 1970 to 1974, he raced a fuel altered, a top fuel dragster, a Vega-bodied funny car, and a rear-engine top fuel dragster, and they all were named "Panic." His best showing in all his nitro-powered cars was his Panic fuel altered, which was also a huge fan favorite in SoCal fuel altered racing.

Less than stellar was "Blazin" Gary Hazen's effort in top fuel in 1971. His Dennis Watson built top fueler never lived up to its potential. Here, at Bakersfield, photographers Jere Alhadeff (left) and Tim Marshall (right) console Hazen after his top fuel had problems and lost fire. All was not bad for Hazen, as his Vega funny car was featured on a T-shirt that was sold worldwide by Roach Studios in Worthington, Ohio, in 1972.

John Keeling and Jerry Clayton's California Charger top fuel dragster was the most beautiful top fuel dragster ever to grace a drag strip in Southern California. It was a true show-and-go top fuel dragster; the Revell model people thought so too and did a model kit of the fueler. Rick Ramsey left top gas and drove the top fueler for Keeling and Clayton. In 1970, the trio took home top fuel honors at the first NHRA Supernationals in Ontario, California. Along with their top fuel dragster, they also raced a Ford Pinto–bodied funny car and then a Ford Mustang–bodied funny car. Their funny cars were just as beautiful as their top fuel dragster.

The Allen family parked its two potent junior fuel dragsters and went top fuel racing in 1970. Les Allen was given the nod to drive the family's fueler, and he was no stranger to the winner's circle. When he drove the family's "Wasp" junior fueler, he won 85 out of 86 races and appeared in the final round. Here, at Irwindale, Allen got a face full of hot oil from the Praying Mantis engine; no worries as he got stopped okay. With that much oil on him, he will never rust.

San Diego's Ted Inque named his top fuel dragster "Wild Thing." In this photograph at OCIR in 1971, Inque and his fueler live up to that name with three giant wheelstands that destroyed the chassis and front end. It was a long tow back to San Diego for Inque and his bent top fuel dragster.

The 1971 NHRA Winternationals at Pomona, California, saw the debut of a one-of-a-kind top fuel dragster. Jim Busby and Bob Burnard's twin-engine top fuel dragster utilized two aluminum dual overhead camshaft (DOHC) Ford engines, equipped with 255s with Hilborn injectors. Also featured were sand-formed stainless-steel headers and a 210-inch Don Long chassis. The car was finished off with a Tom Hanna body and Cerny/Kelly paint. "Surfer" Hank Westmoreland was the driver chosen by Busby, but unfortunately, the car never performed and quickly vanished from SoCal, never to be seen again.

The Hot Wheels/Mattel racing program expanded in 1971 to include a top fuel dragster for Don Prudhomme and Tom McEwen. These cars were featured in television commercials and playsets nationwide. Every little boy wanted a Snake versus Mongoose playset, and Mattel was so happy to provide them. Mattel went heavy into drag racing with the sponsorship of two funny cars and two top fuel dragsters for 1971. The Mattel sponsorship was considered the best in all of drag racing in the early 1970s.

SoCal's Mike Kuhl had Steve Carbone, Bill Tidwell, and Dick Rosburg all having drive time in his top fuel dragster, but in mid-1971 when Rosburg left, he had no driver for his fueler. This was about the same time Carl Olson had crashed the Olson and Bowman top fueler at Fremont. A new top fuel team was formed with Kuhl and Olson—"Da Fast Guys." The pair became fast friends and raced together for the next five or more years in the front-engine and rear-engine top fuel class.

The biggest win for Don Prudhomme's "Hot Wheels" top fuel dragster came in 1971 at the Mattel Hot Wheels Nationals at Fremont, California. Mike Snively, not Prudhomme, drove the fueler to a final-round victory over Rick Ramsey and the California Charger top fuel dragster. This was the only major win for that car, as it was retired soon after this win and was replaced with a rear-engine top fuel dragster.

Swimming pool contractor Jack Raitt's final venture into SoCal top fuel was the Syndicate II top fuel dragster. The team of Raitt, Caldwell, and Forthman put together the twin-engine Syndicate II; it was the heaviest and biggest top fuel dragster in SoCal at 2,500 pounds with a 250-inch RCS chassis. It had twin 354 Chrysler Hemis, and the total cost of the car was $32,000. Phil "Boy Wonder" Ditmars drove a twin-engine beast that was featured on the cover of the October 1971 issue of *Drag Racing* magazine.

Ted Cyr won top fuel eliminator at the Bakersfield March Meet in 1960 while driving the Cyr and Hopper top fuel dragster. Eleven years later, and once again, Ted Cyr went top fuel racing, this time with Flip Schofield. The pair purchased the former Abbott and Lee Shifter top fuel dragster, and with their sponsor Escondido Auto Parts, they were ready to race in top fuel SoCal style. The team made the switch to a rear-engine top fueler in 1972.

"Lil John" Buttera was well known for building funny car chassis and handcrafting parts out of blocks of aluminum in the early 1970s. Before he relocated to Southern California from his native Wisconsin, he did build dragster chassis; in fact, he raced in junior fuel with one of his dragster chassis. Then in 1971, former junior fuel racer Don Ewald raced the last dragster chassis built by Buttera in top fuel. Ewald did so on a shoestring budget, with Fred Smith tuning the car's 392 Chrysler Hemi.

Larry Dixon drove the Larry and Pat Dixon top fuel dragster, which was the last front-engine top fueler to win the Las Vegas Open. The 1971 race featured both front-engine and rear-engine top fuel dragsters, and Dixon waded through a stellar field of SoCal top fuelers that included Jeb Allen (pictured on the far side). Dixon defeated the new rear-engine top fuel dragster of Jim Brissette and Bob Noice in the final to win top fuel eliminator.

For almost 10 years, TV Tommy Ivo owned and drove front-engine top fuel dragsters. At the end of 1971, Ivo made the switch to a rear-engine top fuel dragster. Of course, being the ultimate showman, his new car was a show-and-go beauty. Ivo never missed a beat and kept touring the United States, collecting motel room keys and stopping at every Howard Johnson's restaurant to gobble up those delicious fried clam strips.

The last-ever top gas eliminator was run at the 1971 NHRA Supernationals in Ontario, California. Kenny Ellis in Larry Van Unen's twin-engine dragster beat Ohio's Jim Bucher in the final to claim top gas eliminator. But Van Unen's car failed to pass tech inspection after the race, so Bucher was awarded the win. With the end of top gas, the car was sold to Bruce Lidtke and turned into a twin-engine top fuel dragster for 1972, with Kenny Ellis driving. Lidtke repainted the car and put a full body on it; the twin-engine fueler turned many heads while racing but that did not win any races.

With the end of top gas in 1971, many top gas racers quit racing or went top fuel racing. One of those who went top fuel racing was blower builder Larry Bowers. At the end of 1970, Bowers had a brand-new top fuel dragster ready to go racing. He took his new car out to OCIR for testing, and the first few shakedown runs were promising. On the third run, Bowers got more traction than he wanted with his new front-engine fueler and performed a back flip or a blowover with his new race car. He walked away from the now-destroyed fueler. The car pictured is Bowers's second new car, with Kenny Safford at the controls. Bowers returned to driving an all-new rear-engine canopied top fueler in mid-1972.

The 1971 version of the Schultz and Glenn top fuel dragster was a big winner for the team. Don Tuttle built the chassis, and Bill Schultz did the engine with Gerry "the Hunter" Glenn behind the wheel. They were owners of the last front-engine top fuel dragster to win the NHRA World Championship. That took place at Amarillo, Texas, in 1971, and they beat a red-lighting Don Garlits in the final for top fuel honors. Garlits was driving his all-new rear-engine top fuel dragster at the event.

Moving from top gas to top fuel in 1971 was San Diego's Dave Russell. Russell had some success racing on the AHRA top fuel circuit around the United States. Russell's top fueler was a test car for his business of race car plumbing, fuel lines, and more. His products could be found across the country on all types of race and street cars. He did make the change to a rear-engine top fuel dragster in 1972.

Santa Barbara's Arly Langlo was top fuel's quickest and fastest postal worker. Langlo raced his "Zip Code" top fueler only in SoCal. Langlo raced on a very tight budget and was a welcome sight at SoCal top fuel events. He did build a rear-engine top fuel dragster for 1973. This was a great move for him because all his fires were behind him now.

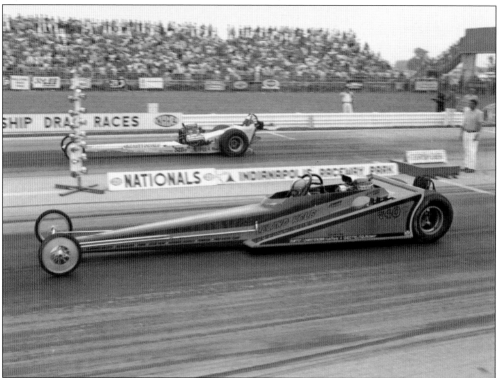

The rear-engine revolution hit SoCal in 1971, and one of the first on board with the rear-engine design was Leland Kolb. Kolb's venture into the rear-engine revolution was his Polish Lotus, a wedge-bodied top fuel dragster. The design looked like it could work, so other racers built similar fuelers; Chris Karamesines, Pancho Rendon, Dan Olson, and Don Prudhomme all built wedge clones. Unfortunately, the design proved too heavy to compete in top fuel racing. Kolb sold his Lotus to the team of Sterling, Prock, and Brown. They removed the wedge body and went racing with Frank Prock driving. Chris Karamesines removed his wedge body to race without the wedge, and Prudhomme did the same. Rendon's car was destroyed in a crash at the 1971 NHRA US Nationals at Indy, and Olson's car just disappeared.

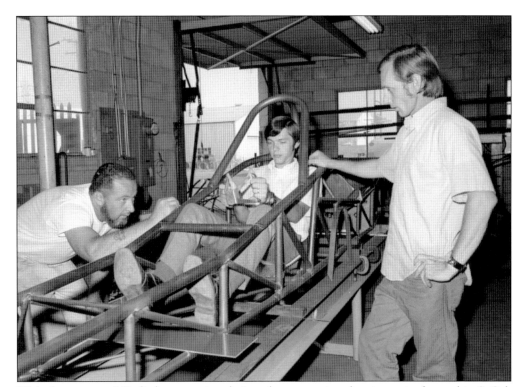

With the success of Garlits's rear-engine design, the rear-engine chassis was in demand in SoCal. Woody Gilmore's shop was a mecca of racers trying to get a rear-engine car built. Mike Kuhl and Carl Olson were one of the first teams to have Gilmore built them a rear-engine chassis. Gilmore is on the left taking measurements while Olson is being fitted for the cockpit, and Mike Kuhl on the right watches his new car come to life. The car proved to be a big winner, as the team of Kuhl and Olson won the 1972 NHRA Winternationals at Pomona, California.

During the summer of 1971, Tom "Mongoose" McEwen was still racing his Mattel Hot Wheels top fuel dragster. However, it was not for long, as he would sell the car to Van Iderstine's speed shop in New Jersey. There, the car was repainted and lettered and then went top fuel racing on the East Coast. Art Marshall was at the controls as the car won the 1972 NHRA Le Grandnational in Montreal, Canada. That win was the last one ever for a front-engine top fuel dragster at an NHRA national event.

One of the last front-engine top fuel dragsters to run in SoCal was the "TNT Special" of Charlie Tolbert and Tom Tolar. It was in 1972 at Irwindale when things went very wrong for the TNT gang with a huge engine explosion and fire. The force of the explosion blew the engine out of the car and made it very interesting for driver Tom Tolar. Tolar, being a longtime top fuel driver, got the engine-less fueler stopped right side up. Tolar was not hurt, but Charlie Tolbert's engine died that day. They built a rear-engine fueler in the coming year.

SoCal's Chuck Tanko went top fuel racing in a big way in 1971. He built and sponsored with his Speed Equipment World a state-of-the-art top fuel dragster. The long yellow beauty was one of the first rear-engine top fuel dragsters to run in SoCal. Kenny Ellis drove Tanko's 392 Chrysler-powered fueler, but the car never lived up to expectations. Tanko parked his top fueler after one season and went funny car racing with ex-top fuel racer Jim Nicoll.

Another team in the rear-engine top fuel race was Danekas, Banks, and Bowman. With the success of Don Garlits's rear-engine fueler, they put their car together in one month. Their one-month wonder was driven by Ron Banks and tuned by Marc Danekas. After a dismal year, the team split up, and Marc Danekas teamed with Oklahoma top fuel racer Marvin Graham to campaign the "TR-3 Resin Glaze Special" out of SoCal.

Hurst's golden shifter girl Linda Vaughn was a huge fan of SoCal top fuel racing since her first appearance at the 1966 *Hot Rod* magazine championships in Riverside, California. In this photograph, she tries out her friend Barry Setzer's Vega funny car driver's cockpit. Vaughn was such a huge fan of SoCal top fuel racing that on December 2, 1972, she married SoCal top fuel driver Bill Tidwell.

Don Prudhomme's switch to a rear-engine top fuel car came in 1971 with this wedge-style fueler. Prudhomme quickly realized that the car was too heavy to compete with the wedge body on it. About midway through 1971, he removed the wedge body, and things got better for him. His next rear-engine car, "the Feather," proved to be a real winner for him and was feared by other top fuel racers nationwide.

In 1972, Barry Setzer and John Buttera thought they were introducing the top fuel dragster of the future, a monocoque-style chassis/body built by Buttera. The car had the best that Setzer's checkbook could dole out. An Ed Pink engine powered the sleek candy-red top fueler, and Pat Foster was named the driver of the future fueler. The car was taken to OCIR for midweek testing, all under hush-hush conditions. Foster made two ill-handling shut-off passes; on the third run, the car stood on its tail and about blew over. Foster reeled the car in as it slammed to the racing surface. The monocoque chassis/body was heavily damaged. They abandoned the car in Buttera's shop until it was sold to rocket-car racers Russell Mendez and Ramon Alvarez. Mendez was killed in a rocket dragster crash in the mid-1970s. The car ended up being restored by Don Garlits, and it now resides in the Don Garlits Museum of Drag Racing in Ocala, Florida.

The very last gasp of the SoCal front-engine top fuel dragster was owned and driven by Dan Horan. It ran in Tulsa, Oklahoma, at the PRO race in 1973. Horan tried a little too hard to qualify his very outdated top fuel dragster, and the result was a huge blower explosion at the finish line. Horan was not hurt, but his wallet took a big hit. Fast forward to 2021, when Dan Horan Jr. won the Bakersfield March Meet in his retro front-engine top fuel dragster with a 6.07 ET at 233 miles per hour.

As the sport of drag racing entered the 1990s, restoring old top fuel dragsters became extremely popular. NHRA and "the Good Guys" each started to hold nostalgic drag racing events in California. Restored and retro cars were built for these events and young and old fans came out in force to see these cars race once again. At NorCal's Sears Point Raceway in 1994 at the Good Guys nostalgia event, it was SoCal versus NorCal, with SoCal's Art Chrisman (nearside) wheeling the fully restored Chrisman Brothers and Cannon top fueler versus NorCal's Mike McLennan driving the restored Champion Speed Shop twin-engine dragster. It did not matter who won, as the tire-smoking show was worth the price of admission.

In 1967, Wild Bill Alexander set a low ET at 7.19 with the Plueger Bros. and Alexander top fuel dragster at the Bakersfield March Meet. Thirty-three years later, Alexander won the Bakersfield March Meet in his nostalgia top fuel dragster. This was Wild Bill's biggest win in his many years as top fuel dragster driver.

Mike Sorokin and the Surfers top fuel dragster took home top fuel honors at the 1966 Bakersfield March Meet. Forty-four years later, his son Adam Sorokin drove Mike Fuller's retro top fuel dragster to top fuel honors at the Bakersfield March Meet in 2010. Adam and Fuller also won the 2019 Bakersfield March Meet, beating Jim Murphy in the final round.

Mendy "Nitro Kitty" Fry was the first woman to run over 250 miles per hour in a nostalgia retro top fuel dragster at 251.32 miles per hour for a 5.95 ET. She was driving the High-Speed Motorsports top fuel dragster in 2009. Fry is the seventh member of the 250-miles-per-hour club and defeated Jim Murphy for top fuel honors at Bakersfield's March Meet in 2017. Then in 2018, she set a low ET at 5.73 and then ran a 5.60 ET at 261.42 miles per hour to set the record for nostalgia top fuel dragsters. (Photograph by Bob Brown.)

The saga of Winkel, Trapp, and Glenn must be told. NorCal's Ray Monteago bought the car from Kent Fuller, who had purchased it from Ron Winkel, one of the original owners. The car was lengthened and ended up being raced by Ray and Jim Lind in NorCal. Then the car was sold to Louis Poole, who had Roy Brizo put it back to its original length. Poole turned and sold the car to Jon Barrett in Oklahoma. Barrett put a blown Hemi engine in it and ran it at Nation Drag Racing Association (NDRA) nostalgic events. Then during the 1990s, Barrett traded the car to Bill Pitts for the original Shelby Super Snake top fuel chassis. Pitts restored the car back to its original form and displayed it at nostalgic events on the West Coast.

When the nostalgia craze hit drag racing, it consumed Mike Kuhl. Kuhl had sold his front-engine top fuel dragster to Dick Thorn in 1972. Thorn renamed the car "Plum Crazy" and ran it a few times in 1972 before selling the car to Dick Krieger, who ran it with a small block Chevy engine with carburetors for bracket racing. After the car had been lost for almost two decades, Kuhl found Krieger and the former Kuhl and Olson top fuel dragster. Kuhl made a deal for the top fueler and took it home that same day. Money, sweat, and time produced a perfectly restored top fuel dragster that Kuhl could be proud of when displayed at nostalgic events.

The two largest gatherings of restored and replica top fuel dragsters take place at the Bakersfield Hot Rod reunion in the month of October. Their cackle fest features about 44 top fuel cars, all cackling their engines while lined up down the Bakersfield quarter-mile. Steve Gibbs's Nitro Revival takes place at Irwindale raceway in November. Gibbs features over 70 restored and replica cars cackling their engines on the Irwindale one-eighth mile. Both are premiere events for restored and replica top fuel dragsters of drag racing's golden era of top fuel racing.

The very last front-end top fuel dragster from the golden era of SoCal top fuel racing was the former Bill Simpson Sky-Jacker. The car ended up in England owned and driven by Mickey Naylor and renamed "the Medicine Man." Here, in 1978, is the beginning of the end of Naylor's top fuel dragster. Naylor went into a giant wheelstand while racing at Santa Pod; the fifth wheel broke off the car as it headed skyward. Naylor and his fueler blew over as the result of losing the fifth wheel, destroying the last of the former SoCal top fuel dragsters. Naylor was not injured and did not return to top fuel racing.

The onset of the rear-engine top fuel dragster proved to be a great breakthrough for safety and performance. Pictured is Larry Bowers having a massive clutch failure in his rear-engine top fuel dragster in 1972. Thankfully, Bowers was not injured in the explosion. Five years earlier, Mike Sorokin was killed from the same type of clutch failure while driving Tony Waters's front-engine top fuel car. The rear-engine design that resulted was a lifesaver for many a top fuel dragster driver of the future.

DISCOVER THOUSANDS OF LOCAL HISTORY BOOKS FEATURING MILLIONS OF VINTAGE IMAGES

Arcadia Publishing, the leading local history publisher in the United States, is committed to making history accessible and meaningful through publishing books that celebrate and preserve the heritage of America's people and places.

Find more books like this at
www.arcadiapublishing.com

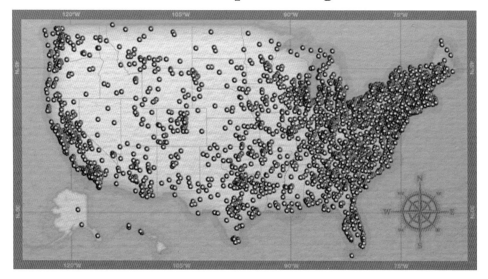

Search for your hometown history, your old stomping grounds, and even your favorite sports team.

Consistent with our mission to preserve history on a local level, this book was printed in South Carolina on American-made paper and manufactured entirely in the United States. Products carrying the accredited Forest Stewardship Council (FSC) label are printed on 100 percent FSC-certified paper.

MADE IN THE